Gilbert and Marianna

with love from

the author

Bill Magan

An Irish Boyhood

An Irish Boyhood

William Magan

William Magan

The Pentland Press Limited
Edinburgh • Cambridge • Durham • USA

© William Magan 1996

First published in 1996 by
The Pentland Press Ltd.
1 Hutton Close
South Church
Bishop Auckland
Durham

British Library Cataloguing in Publication Data.
A catalogue record for this book is available
from the British Library.

ISBN 1 85821 415 7

Typeset by CBS, Felixstowe, Suffolk
Printed and bound by Antony Rowe Ltd., Chippenham

For

MAXINE

CONTENTS

ACKNOWLEDGEMENTS

I must first express my gratitude to Maxine, my wife, for her inspiration, her encouragement, her patience with my necessarily long periods of solitary writing, for her subsequent meticulous examination of the text and for her many useful suggestions.

I am grateful, too, to Nancy Christopherson for editing the text, and for her invaluable suggestions and comments.

And I am no less grateful to Mrs Alice Robinson for her skill in turning my none too tidy manuscript into a neat typescript.

W.M.T. Magan

INTRODUCTION

This book recounts my Irish boyhood some eighty years ago, when life was unlike the way we live today. It was a mainly horse-drawn era with very few motor cars and no aeroplanes. Our dwellings, too, seldom had either electricity or house telephones – a very different Ireland from the prosperous modern country which we know now.

That charming Irish writer, Anita Leslie, has said that an Irish childhood does something to your toes: they grow roots. I hope that this story of my own Irish childhood will help to illustrate why that should be, and why, although I have lived the whole of my adult life outside Ireland – except for visits – I still feel that I am essentially the boy who grew up there.

Chapter 1

The Background to my Early Life (1)

I was born in Southern Ireland on the outskirts of the splendid market town of Athlone in County Westmeath, and I was born into an Ascendancy family at a time when the Ascendancy was about to decline into near oblivion; at a time, too, when the whole of Ireland was a part of the United Kingdom. I was therefore born both British and Irish. And it so happened that my parents and, in the upshot I and my brother and sisters, became the victims of discord that existed within the Ascendancy. That I shall come to in the next chapter.

The Ascendancy became fully established in the last decade of the seventeenth century when the native Irish Catholic forces were finally routed by the mainly Protestant English settler army representing the English Crown which at that time became invested in William III and his wife Mary. The Battle of the Boyne in 1690 is the best known event leading to the victory of the Protestant Ascendancy, though it was in fact neither the last nor the most important encounter between the two sides in the so-called Jacobite war.

At that time, land-owning was the prerequisite of power and the Ascendancy, which consisted of about fifteen hundred large land-owning, mainly English settler families wielded all the power in Ireland that Whitehall would allow.

The Ascendancy comprised three sorts of families. There were the few remnants of the old Celtic chieftainly families whose lands had been the property of their tribes and septs for two thousand years. Then there were, similarly, not many old English settler Catholic families who had settled in Ireland and obtained their estates there during the four hundred years between the Welsh-Norman invasion of Ireland in 1169 and the end of the sixteenth century. But the great majority of the Ascendancy families were the scions of Protestant land-owning families in England who were adventurous enough to obtain land by fair means or foul in Ireland and to settle there in its disturbed state in the seventeenth century. Many of them were murdered, particularly in the insurrection of 1641. What the Ascendancy came to amount to was the colonial garrison of a country strategically very important to Britain which was threatened by hostile Catholic powers, France and Spain, who, had they succeeded in their attempts to dominate Ireland, would have closed England's vital sea lines of communication to the Atlantic Ocean, and thence to the world. But the Protestant Ascendancy families had also come to own most of the best land in Ireland, which remained a grievance with the dispossessed native Irish Catholic community.

England and Ireland were at that time two Kingdoms having one monarch, the King or Queen of both England and Ireland. The Irish had their own Parliament in Dublin, a House of Commons and a House of Lords. When the Protestant establishment in Ireland became confirmed in power at the end of the seventeenth century, the Irish Parliament became exclusively Protestant, with the House of Lords much under the influence of Protestant bishops. Not only did Catholics become excluded from both Houses, but also they were not even allowed a vote throughout almost the whole of the eighteenth century, when the Ascendancy held down the Catholic majority under an extensive code of disgraceful penal enactments, known as the Penal Laws, designed to suppress the Catholic religion and to render all Catholics little better than ignorant peasants or even paupers.

These dreadful Catholic handicaps underwent gradual amelioration during the latter part of the eighteenth century and the early years of the nineteenth century. By the Act of Union of 1801, Ireland became in effect a province of England. The Houses of Parliament were closed down. Parliamentary constituencies were created in Ireland which elected members to Parliament at Westminster; Irishmen of every denomination had the vote; Irish commoners of whatever religion were elected to the Westminster Parliament, and Irish peers could take their seats in the House of Lords.

By the mid nineteenth century the characteristics of the Ascendancy had changed in a number of ways. It remained largely, but no longer exclusively, Protestant. It had been joined by some of the old mainly Catholic Celtic chieftainly families, and the mainly Catholic settlers from England who had gone to Ireland between the twelfth and the sixteenth centuries, and who, by one means or another, had survived the suppression of the eighteenth century. It now sent representatives to the Westminster Parliament and, because it still owned the bulk of Irish lands, it had considerable local authority, but its minority membership of the Westminster Parliament gave it virtually no power over the overall government of Ireland.

The Ascendancy at rest

The Ascendancy at rest

In the seventeenth century, England looked upon the Irish as savages, and regarded themselves as superior people to the Irish. The old twelfth to sixteenth century English settlers found the Irish and their customs acceptable. They married Irish girls, adopted Irish dress and customs, took to the Irish language, and were said to have become more Irish than the Irish. The seventeenth century English settlers however evolved differently. As generation after generation was brought up in Ireland, so they ceased to be English and became Irish *sui generis*, at the same time owing a fierce loyalty to the English Crown. They did not adopt Irish customs. On the contrary, they introduced English customs into Ireland, and made English the language of the land. The Ascendancy saw themselves as a master race. This was not an intellectual position. It was innate – an inherent attitude of mind. If you were a member of the Ascendancy you knew that you were born superior. It was, you believed, a God-given condition, not man-made.

But, as the nineteenth century wore on, there became an increasing understanding between the mainly Protestant landlords and the Catholic natives, the majority of whom were peasants, and this developed into mutual respect and amity, and even much affection. The Irish were used to the master race condition. The old Celtic chiefs had been a master race. In the days when the chiefs ruled Ireland, no man could become a chief unless he descended from a chieftainly family. He was born superior simply by his birth. In consequence, the Ascendancy landlords, living in the big house, inherited the respect which had been accorded to the chiefs and became known to the Catholic peasantry as the 'gintry' (gentry) and the 'quality', while the Protestant clergyman was 'Yer riverence', and the Catholic peasantry valued and enjoyed the big house to which they could turn for protection, advice and support, and which gave the lead in many aspects of life.

In relation to the mutual respect and liking which the big house and the cottage people had for each other by the latter part of the nineteenth century, Stephen Gwynn wrote this about his upbringing in rural Donegal, twenty-five miles from the nearest railway station:

The Ascendancy at rest

The best thing which I learnt was to be as easily at home in an Irish cottage as in the houses of my own class. For in Ireland we recognised class as a matter of course; and as a result well-bred people in cottage or big house were never class conscious.

In a sense that was misleading. Class conscious, or caste conscious, is what they were, but they were not class-antagonistic.

However, the undercurrents of change were there. The defeat of the French at the Battle of Waterloo had removed the threat of an invasion of Ireland by a powerful hostile Catholic power, and the Home Rule bills at the turn of the nineteenth/twentieth centuries, although they failed in Parliament, were a sign of England's weakening will to continue her rule in Ireland. The spirit of the ancient Picto-Celtic Ireland was in the ascendant; the Ascendancy was on the wane. It had depended for finance largely on rents from its large estates, but it was no longer needed by England as a colonial garrison to underwrite British rule in Ireland, so England gave it the *coup de grâce* – the Wyndham Act of 1903 – five years before my birth. The Act made it mandatory for land owners to sell to their tenants, if they wished to buy them, their rented farms. By this means the Ascendancy landlords were to be stripped of their estates, and the land was to be returned to the native Catholic Irish. Land is an Irishman's love. All that was to be left to an Ascendancy landlord was his demesne lands or home farm which was in hand. That would not be enough to maintain the big house, and thus many of the Ascendancy families would be unable to survive. It took more than twenty years to complete this process.

Politically, too, the native Catholic Irish were being led towards independence. Curiously, a number of their most prominent political leaders were themselves members of the Protestant Ascendancy – for instance, Wolfe Tone, Lord Edward Fitzgerald, Robert Emmet, Charles Stewart Parnell and Constance Gore-Booth who became better known as the Countess Markievicz. There was also sporadic violence aimed at achieving Catholic independence.

The third Irish Home Rule Bill passed through Parliament in September 1914 and entered the Statute Book but, because of the outbreak of World War One a month earlier, was not then implemented. It was not until December 1921, and after two outbreaks of violence – the Easter Rising of 1916 and 'The Troubles', so called, of 1919-21 – that independence within the Commonwealth was granted to the twenty-six mainly Catholic counties of Southern Ireland which chose to be called the Irish Free State. Six of the former nine counties of Ulster, known as Northern Ireland, which were mainly Protestant, became an internally self-governing province of the United Kingdom.

After the twenty-six counties of Southern Ireland became independent, the Ascendancy in that part of Ireland lost all its authority and now, near the end of the twentieth century, not more than twenty per cent of the old Ascendancy families still live in Ireland.

W.B. Yeats said of the Ascendancy that it was 'one of the great stocks of Europe'. Its members had their defects, but against that they had great virtues. They were hardy and capable people. They led mostly open air lives, both the men and the girls, riding, walking, fishing, managing boats, climbing mountains, farming, and acquiring outdoor skills generally. They rose early and worked hard, and were capable of tolerating any discomfort. At the same time, they were not philistines. Thackaray, after his visit to Ireland, said of them:

> Nor am I in the least disposed to sneer at gentlemen who like sporting and talk about it: for I believe that the conversation of a dozen foxhunters is just as clever as that of a similar number of merchants, barristers or literary men.

In consequence of their hardy upbringing, the young men of the Ascendancy became a major source of recruitment of officers for the British armed services. They produced a quite disproportionate number of British military leaders, of whom the Duke of Wellington was only one; and, at a lower level, they officered a splendid array of Irish regiments in the British Army, the rank and file, except for the Ulster Units, being Catholic to a man, and splendidly vigorous, valiant and loyal soldiers.

No mention of the Irish Ascendancy should overlook its great wealth of men of letters. Furthermore, the Ascendancy produced many of those who officered and administered the British Colonial Empire. At home in Ireland, too, they were doers who gave Ireland a great network of railways, roads and canals to facilitate her rural and industrial growth which they also promoted in other ways. That is not to suggest that the native Catholic Irish could not have done these things for themselves or that they did not contribute extensively, but so long as the Protestant Ascendancy dominated Ireland, the native Catholics were largely relegated to a secondary role.

That briefly pictures the general, social and political Irish Ascendancy into which I was born and which was the background to my boyhood life. My parents continued to see themselves as having been born superior, and members of the master race, and some of that must have rubbed off on me. And was it because of the tradition of young Ascendancy men to become officers in the British armed forces that I, as a boy of fifteen, made up my mind to become an officer in the British Indian Army?

Chapter 2

The Background to my Early Life (2)

When, after my parents' death, our Irish family home, Killyon Manor, Co. Meath was dismantled, a quantity of documents came to light, which revealed in detail the traumatic, dramatic and cruel events surrounding my parents' marriage. The dramatis personae of this hideously tragic affair, which was sorely to affect my parents' married life, and to blight a part of my young life, were my maternal grandfather and grandmother, Assheton and Florence Biddulph, and my mother and father, Kathleen Biddulph and Shaen Magan. The Lady Macbeth of the tragedy was my grandmother, Florence Biddulph, wanting in natural affection, and inflexible of wicked will:

Come all you spirits
That tend on mortal thoughts, unsex me here:
And fill me, from the crown to th' toe, top-full of direst cruelty;
make thick my blood, stop up the access and passage to remorse,
that no compunctious visiting of nature shake my fell purpose . . .

The discord in the Ascendancy which manifested itself in this case arose from the difference between my father and my mother's mother. He was a warm eccentric Irishman. She was a chilly English woman, hidebound with upper-class Victorian conventionality. Moreover, there was a difference between the two families.

My father's family was not a settler family. The Magans descended from Celtic chiefs and can trace their Celtic background to the first century AD, and were, therefore, at the more Irish end of the Anglo-Irish Ascendancy.

My mother's family, the Irish Biddulphs, were an Anglo-Norman family, tracing their origin to the standard bearer to William the Conqueror, Ormus le Guidon, who was granted lands at Biddulph in Staffordshire from which the family took its name, and in the seventeenth century a member of the family, John Biddulph, went to Ireland and obtained an estate at Rathrobin in the King's County (now Offaly). Not untypically, he was murdered, but his son carried on the line at Rathrobin.

My mother's father, Assheton Biddulph, was a famous Master of Foxhounds who owned and hunted the King's County hounds throughout most of his adult life. Her mother was Florence Boothby, daughter of an English land-owning family of noble Danish descent whose name is linked with the soil of England at Boothby Pagnell. She was, therefore, at the more Anglicised end of the Anglo-Irish Ascendancy.

She was a formidable woman, a strong character, a fine horse-woman, a good musician, and much given to good and useful works particularly for the girls and young women in the Irish countryside in which she was living. But she had a heart of stone. Hers was a background of disciplined, tightly self-controlled, conventional, English elegance set in a bedrock of stoical, uncomplaining endurance. The males of her family were receiving their education at Eton and Oxford and Cambridge, ready, if necessary, to become pro-consuls of the British Empire which was then at its zenith. According to my mother, her father, Assheton Biddulph, always followed his wife's lead. In matters other than hunting she called the tune.

By contrast with Florence Biddulph and her English ethos, my father, Shaen Magan, never went to school and never left Ireland until he was grown up. He was educated by a succession of Church of Ireland parsons, governesses and tutors. He was never, therefore, subject to school discipline or to the competition of his peers. Moreover, as the youngest child in his family, he was much spoilt by a doting mother and four older sisters. His mother's father, his maternal grandfather, was a clergyman, and his maternal great-grandfather was a bishop. His upbringing, therefore, assured that he was strongly imbued with Christian principles and morality. But he had superficial foibles which could mask his essential soundness.

He had a marked personality and a strong voice, and was noisy and exceedingly talkative. He was lacking in reticence, deficient in modesty, conversationally self-assertive, sometimes boastful, and more than a little prone to hyperbole and colourful embroidery and exaggeration. He was nevertheless kind and helpful to his relations and his friends. He was excellent and interesting company. He had a good brain and a quick mind, and he was much liked by people in all walks of life in Ireland where he was understood. But my grandmother-to-be, Florence Biddulph, did not understand him and did not like him.

He came to know the Biddulph family very well. There is an indication in the surviving papers that he was helping Assheton Biddulph with some project or other as throughout his life he helped many others. Giving such assistance gratis was one of his great satisfactions in life. No matter how difficult or complex the task, his self-confidence always urged him to take it on. Moreover, in this case, he no doubt got on well with Assheton Biddulph who was himself a fairly eccentric Irishman to whom my father would not have seemed outlandish. At all events, the Biddulph visitors book shows that he stayed at the Biddulph home, Moneyguyneen, near Rathrobin in the King's County, thirteen times between November 1902 and September 1903.

The Biddulph family consisted of four girls and one boy, Bertie, the youngest. My father fell in love with the eldest daughter, Kathleen, and it was on his thirteenth visit to Moneyguyneen that they decided to marry, but when my father asked the Biddulph parents for their consent, they declined to give it there and then on the grounds that he was rather young (he was twenty-three and Kathleen, my mother-to-be, a year younger) and on the need to be sure that he would be able to afford marriage.

The truth was that Florence Biddulph did not want this marriage to take place and hoped to scupper it on the grounds of an inadequate financial situation.

My father was too smart to be caught out like that. The Biddulphs were dealing with a clever man who was formidable in matters of

Kathleen Magan, née Biddulph, my mother, in court dress when presented to
Edward VII

business. He therefore lost no time in inviting Assheton Biddulph to a meeting with his stockbroker in his Dublin office, where his financial situation would be made clear in detail. The meeting duly took place and it was made clear to Assheton that my father could well afford to marry.

This placed the Biddulphs in a dilemma, which was increased by the fact that my father's senile father died two months later leaving my father heir to his inheritance which included the 3,500 acre estate where he lived in County Roscommon. They could still fall back on his youthfulness as a reason to hold up the betrothal, but they did something else. They did not invite him to Moneyguyneen for the next four months, hoping that things would cool off between him and Kathleen. At the end of that period, one of my father's sisters, Rachel, who was a friend of Mrs Biddulph's and who was engaged in the same sort of good works for local girls, spent ten days with the Biddulphs at Moneyguyneen. During her visit she told Mrs Biddulph that not only was my father quite well enough off to marry, but that he was also a very mature, competent and experienced young man who had, since he was seventeen years of age, during his father's long years of senility, been running the estate and family affairs generally, as well as earning his own living.

This left the Biddulphs with no grounds for refusing his engagement to my mother and they must have told my mother so because ten days after Rachel's visit she sent my father a telegram saying, 'All right. Come any day, Kathleen.'

The day of that telegram was a hunting day, and we know from the Hunt scrapbook that my mother had kept since she was a child, that she herself was hunting that day. It was a special day. Her father was not hunting his own hounds. It was an annual event, an invitation day to the neighbouring Ormond Hunt to bring their hounds to hunt the King's County country. Colonel Harrison, their Master, brought his dog pack. Hounds met at a house at the foot of the Slieve Bloom mountains where the generous host gave welcome refreshment to the field before they moved off.

It was a successful day. There was a long fast run in the morning, and by late afternoon hounds had followed a fox high up into the mountains. It was February, and the cold light of the winter afternoon was fading so, with a fog-clad mountain looming ahead of them, hounds were called off. There was still a long jog home with collars turned up against the rain because the day had started 'dark, wet and cheerless'. But it had been a good day for all that. All 'were very pleased with the success of the visiting pack'.

And, especially, I hope my mother was pleased. I hope she was able to enjoy the day with a quiet mind, perhaps with joy in her heart in consequence of the telegram she had posted that morning. I hope so, indeed, because she enjoyed hunting just as much as her father did. She had been his shadow in the hunting field for years. He himself recorded of that day that she 'rode close on the back of her father, so we were "there or thereabouts" throughout the day'. Yes, I sincerely hope they both enjoyed themselves because, although she could not know it then, and he himself must have been equally unsuspecting, it was to prove to be the swan-song of their long hunting, fishing, mountain-walking, and general home and country companionship together. The fates were gathering in the twilight of those fog-clad mountains, poised to descend upon the father and his favourite daughter and, within the week, to shatter their happiness in each other into a thousand fragments, never to be put together again. Spiritually they would never more be 'there or thereabouts' together.

The following day Assheton Biddulph wrote a conciliatory letter to my father welcoming him to marry Kathleen. He was no doubt relieved to be free of the embarrassing situation into which his wife had forced him.

My father then lost no time in making himself available for the formal betrothal ceremony at Moneyguyneen. The day after receiving Assheton Biddulph's letter, he went to the Biddulph home, taking his sister Rachel with him, and on that winter evening of 23 February 1904, there took place by the light of candles, and in the warmth of a blazing log and 'turf' fire, in the presence of the family, the formal commitment of betrothal, with felicitations from all; whereafter, in due course, the household retired for the night in a spirit of mutual good will.

The next day, my father had a *tête-à-tête* with Assheton Biddulph and told him in detail of his own and his mother's and his four sisters' circumstances following his father's death six weeks earlier. Assheton seems not to have understood what my father told him since he formed the opinion that my father was much less well off than he had made himself out to be in his stockbroker's office, and it now seemed that he was not well enough off to marry. This alarmed him and he discussed it with his wife, who concluded that my father had deceived them and that here were formidable grounds for cancelling the engagement and being rid of my father.

It was, of course, a preposterous conclusion. My father had not deceived them, and would never have thought of doing any such devious thing. He was an entirely honest and honourable man; nor could he have done so in the presence of his stockbroker. Moreover, being a clever man, had he wanted to deceive them, he would not have been so foolish as to show his hand before he had got the girl safely wed.

At all events, that evening after dinner, Assheton Biddulph, fuddled with whisky punch and port, as he always was after dinner, saw my father again alone and accused him of deception, said that the engagement must now be cancelled and forced my father to agree not to see or correspond with my mother for a year. Furthermore, he and Rachel must leave the house early next morning so that they should not see Kathleen. This they did, having first signed the visitors book, and neither of them ever saw the Biddulphs again.

Assheton thought a year's separation would be sufficient to quell my parents' ardour for one another, but his wife would not have it. The ban must be for ever. So, the following day, Assheton forced my mother to promise never to see my father again. This was not just for a year, but for life. But Assheton was making a great mistake. If he was a stubborn elderly man, she was a no less stubborn young woman. This undertaking had been extracted from her under duress. Her father had said that if she would not agree he would drink himself to death.

My mother was an exceptionally uncomplicated person. Early in life she established a code of simple rules of conduct and morality to guide and inform and condition every aspect of her life. There was not the least wrinkle of deviousness in her whole character. Living for her was quite straightforward. Things were either right or wrong, good or bad, black or white. She refused to contemplate grey areas. And throughout the whole of this distressing time of her engagement, she remained calm and patient. She knew what was right and stuck resolutely and unmoved – indeed immovable – to it, despite the pressures brought to bear upon her by her parents. And she was a religious person and knew the scriptures. 'Be strong and of good courage.' And, withal she was a sweet and sweet-natured and simple person.

Her father's ultimatum to her failed the test, under her rules. She had given her promise of marriage to my father. That was right and

The Ascendancy were large-scale agriculturalists

good and must stand. Her father had under duress extracted a second promise from her. That was bad and wrong and must be ignored.

At the same time, Assheton wrote to my father telling him that the ban must be for all time, not simply for a year. My father, like my mother, refused to accept this unilateral cancellation of the condition he had entered into. What Assheton had now succeeded in doing was to array my father and mother against him in solemn determination to have their way in due course. In reply to Assheton's letter, therefore, my father gave fair warning that when the year was up he reserved the right to take such steps as were open to him to wed my mother.

Outwardly, the Biddulphs continued to pretend that it was on the grounds of my father not being well enough off that they opposed the marriage. The fact was that he was far from badly off. His father had been extravagant, but there was plenty left. Eventually, when he and my mother married, they had three children in the first four years of marriage. Under the Wyndham Act he had been selling off farms from the estate to tenants, but he had kept a fully stocked farm and his father's house in Roscommon, and he and my mother lived in a commodious Georgian rented house on the outskirts of Athlone, with two paddocks for cows and horses, a walled garden, and outdoor and indoor staff. My mother kept horses and hunted, and my father shot every weekend throughout the winter; he had his own sizeable yacht on Lough Ree, sharing a boatman with his sister Violet, and engaged in yacht racing during summer weekends. He and my mother both fished as much as they could. In addition, his four sisters were provided for financially, and his mother's life interest in a considerable amount of capital enabled her to live in a substantial house, St Marks, large enough for herself and her four daughters, and beautifully situated in seventy acres of parkland overlooking Lough Ree, with an indoor and outdoor staff. The 'short of money' reason for holding up the marriage was simply not going to run for the Biddulphs.

Considering that they were both still quite young, my father and mother showed extraordinary maturity in handling this difficult situation. They acted with great patience and forbearance and went out of their way not to provoke the Biddulph parents. During the year's moratorium they took no steps which might disturb things further. My mother was sent abroad to stay with friends in Portugal in the hope that she would find some distraction there, which she did not. But when she returned, and the year's moratorium came to an end, and the Biddulphs continued to forbid her to have any communication with my father, both she and he began manoeuvres to break the log jam. They both appointed intermediaries between themselves and the Biddulph parents.

My father's intermediary was a friend of his who was also a friend of the Biddulphs. He went to Moneyguyneen and discovered that the Biddulphs had found a new reason for forbidding the marriage – that because of his lack of formal education, my father would be unable to compete in the world. In fact, he was already doing better at his age than many older men. In addition to his private business affairs, the work that he did for the Agricultural Co-operative Movement, which had been set up to help small farmers, carried the rank of a temporary Civil Servant, and, at that time, he received a letter from his Civil Servant boss which contained this:

> I thank you heartily for your co-operation; I hope before long to be able to congratulate you on having attained for yourself a position in the movement which will compensate you for your unselfish efforts to promote a work which alone could have called forth such self-sacrifice as you have invariably shown.

And scraping the barrel for reasons to prevent the marriage, the Biddulphs accused my father of flirting with my mother's next younger sister, Ierne, while at the same time wooing my mother. My father had no difficulty in refuting that. He and Ierne were good friends all their lives, but there was never more to it than that.

My mother's intercession centred on a cousin of her mother's for whom her mother had a high regard, Colonel the Hon. Ulick Roche CB. He was staying at Moneyguyneen. My mother persuaded her parents to let him meet my father, which he did in my father's Dublin office. He liked my father and his report on him was entirely favourable, but the Biddulphs remained unmoved.

My father's intermediary was still in play and found that Assheton Biddulph's argument for forbidding the marriage still was that my father had deceived him at the time of the meeting with his stockbroker. My father, therefore, decided to obtain a report from the stockbroker and, to that end, arranged for his intermediary and another mutual friend of his and the Biddulphs, George Moony of the Doon, to meet the stockbroker and get a full report from him. The meeting took place in the stockbroker's office, towards the end of December 1905, and the stockbroker's report entirely upheld my father's case. George Moony wrote a full report and it was sent to Assheton Biddulph.

His reaction is summed up in one sentence in his reply which is dated 7 January 1906:

> I have read all most carefully and my opinions are quite unaltered.

and in that letter he came as near to telling the truth as the Biddulphs ever were when he wrote:

> I really can't see any further use in discussing the question of money . . . As I have said before, money is a very secondary consideration in this matter.

So it was not lack of money that was the cause of the objection. The truth as to what the real reason was remained unspoken.

My father and mother had now been patient for two years, but to no avail. My father had warned Assheton through George Moony that, if he continued to be obstinate, he, my father, would immediately take the law into his own hands. The time had now come for action, and it was taken so swiftly that my mother and father were married within a fortnight of the receipt of Assheton Biddulph's final letter.

George Moony's house, the Doon, was the chosen rendezvous of the wedding conspirators. Thither went my father with two of his sisters, the oldest, Blossie (Emily Georgina Magan) and the youngest, Violet, on 18 January 1906. And thither on 20 January, George

Moony fetched my mother from the house of friends whom she was visiting for a few days - a common practice at that time. The next day, 21 January, was a Sunday. An invitation was sent to Assheton Biddulph and his wife to come to the Doon where they would have received an invitation to the wedding next day. My father's eldest sister, my Aunt Blossie, kept a diary. Of that day she wrote:

We waited all day for Mr and Mrs Biddulph to come over as they had been invited, but they did not come, but sent a carriage with Miss Baker (a governess) at 5 o'clock with a furious letter to fetch K home, but she would not go.

The Ascendancy was horse-drawn

21

And before going to bed Blossie wrote in her diary:

Almost the longest day I ever spent.

So, that was that. Next day, 22 January 1906, my parents were married, and Blossie wrote in her diary:

Went to bed early and had a good sleep at last.

Having failed to accept the wedding invitation, the Biddulphs were never prepared to see or speak to my father or mother again.

Although my mother eloped, the wedding was a decent affair – not a hole in a corner business. It took place in St Mary's Church in the middle of the ancient, historic town of Athlone.

The best man was a professional friend of my father, Ernest Aldwell. And there were bridesmaids, one of whom was Ernest Aldwell's bride to be. She and Ernest lived to attend my parents' golden wedding celebrations fifty years later.

The ceremony was conducted by the Very Reverend the Dean of Clonmacnoise, Dean Verschoyle-Campbell. The deanery, or rectory as it in fact was, was adjacent to the church and, as a small boy, I recall the dean as a formidable, bearded old man terrifyingly reminiscent of my imaginary picture of the Almighty. The dean had three sons. One of them, William Verschoyle-Campbell, was my godfather. He became a general in the Army and attended my wedding in Delhi, India, in 1940. My other godfather was the conspirator, George Moony.

The deanery had been a home from home for my father throughout his boyhood, and the dean knew him very well, and would not have involved himself in the marriage had he thought there was any reasonable objection to it.

The reason made public by the Biddulphs for their objection to the marriage was the demonstrably false one that my father could not afford it. Some wag wrote a limerick about it:

> There was an old Master of Hounds,
> Whose folly exceeded all bounds,

He went clean off his head,
When his daughter got wed:
And all for a handful of pounds.

Assheton's older brother, Colonel Middleton Biddulph, asked Assheton what he had against my father, whom Middleton liked. Assheton said it was because he hardly knew him. However, shortly after the wedding, Middleton paid a visit to Moneyguyneen. Assheton and his wife were out and, while waiting for their return, Middleton happened to look through the visitors book and saw that my father had been a frequent guest at Moneyguyneen. When Assheton returned, Middleton charged him with the fact that he had said that he hardly knew my father. How was it then that his name was in the visitors book so often? From then on, Middleton, who was well off and had no children, made my mother an allowance and later appointed her his heir.

Of her immediate family, only her next sister, Ierne, showed her any goodwill. At the time of the marriage she was in England, and four days after the wedding she wrote to my mother from London. She explained her dilemma, and said she must stick by her parents, but she ended her letter:

If in the years to come you ever want any kind of help that I can give you, please let me know and I will do all I can wherever I am. I most sincerely hope you will be happy.
Your affectionate sister
Ierne

Clearly, the reason why Assheton and his wife were never prepared to give the real reason for their objection to the marriage was because they were sufficiently conscious that Florence Biddulph's objections might easily be judged to be such a typical act of a particularly offensive brand of English upper class snobbery that it would be impossible for them to divulge it without making themselves look embarrassingly silly. My father had not been to Eton and Cambridge, or, like her own son, to Harrow and Oxford, and was too near the

Irish end of the Anglo-Irish Ascendancy spectrum for her.

I feel that in justice to my parents I must pass judgement on my Biddulph grandparents. From the beginning, my grandmother was determined to frustrate the marriage and, throughout, she used my grandfather as a tool to that end. He should have had enough manliness to stand up to her, but he did not. He went along with her. They accused my father of a deliberate deceit of which he was manifestly not guilty. But they never thought to look for the beam in their own eye. Theirs was the unself-critical, self-righteousness of the scribes and Pharisees. They practised their own deceit in never declaring their real reason for objecting to the match. They would hear no argument, listen to no reason. Prejudice in the beginning, stubborn pride at the end, led them needlessly, and almost unbelievably, to the heartless decision to disown and outlaw their own daughter for ever. They stand revealed as devoid of humility, humanity, compassion, charity, forgiveness and natural affection. What they did to their innocent daughter – for my mother was a simple and innocent person – was a cold-blooded piece of gratuitous wickedness. Their blind prejudice and stubborn pride were far greater wrongs than any charge they could lay against my father.

And did they not think of the consequences of their actions for the family, and for the fabric of the society in which they lived? To create such a breach is to do grievous harm. They caused social strains and embarrassment locally. They never knew their own grandchildren. We, the grandchildren, were deprived of grandparents, and of an uncle and aunts. Because our Magan grandfather had died before we were born, we never knew what it was to have a grandfather. And because my father's only brother had settled in America, we never knew what it was to have an uncle. As young children, we missed the interest and pleasure of all that went on at the Biddulph home, the hounds and hound puppies and the horses, and as older children we would have experienced the great pleasure and satisfaction of climbing the Slieve Bloom mountains, and there would have been all the interesting people working at our grandparents' home whom we would have got to know.

That a grandmother would not wish to see her only grandchildren is almost beyond the bounds of credibility. But my Biddulph grandmother's attitude to us as children was wicked beyond belief. As each of us was born she wished us dead.

There was a moment ripe for reconciliation. Nearly eight years after my parents' marriage, my mother's sister, Ierne, was married on 3 August 1913. Her betrothed, Jack Gould-Adams, was an officer in an Irish line regiment but, although his was an Ascendancy family, he was not good enough, or was too Irish, for Florence Biddulph, and the marriage was forbidden. But Assheton Biddulph's older brother, Middleton Biddulph, stepped in and said that if Assheton and Florence Biddulph were not prepared to agree to the wedding, he, Middleton, would arrange it from his own house, Rathrobin. Assheton and Florence Biddulph capitulated and gave Ierne a full-scale wedding from their own place, Moneyguyneen. I and my two sisters Sheelagh and Mollie were aged seven, five and three years old. We lived only twelve miles from our Biddulph grandparents' home. It could have been arranged for us to attend our Aunt Ierne's wedding as page and bridesmaids, but our Biddulph grandmother would not hear of it. Incredible!

That was the family background into which I was born and in which I was brought up. It was my lot to have a mother with only an unknown and hostile family, and to know only what it was to have my father's family. Fortunately my Magan grandmother and my four Magan aunts took the greatest interest in us as children. My grandmother did not die until I was eighteen, so she and my wonderful aunts were a constantly interesting, lively, and enjoyable influence throughout our childhood.

The extended family of grandparents, aunts, uncles, parents and children has important strengths and influences particularly for the children. If deprived of any part of it, their souls are to that extent impoverished. That more than three-quarters of a century later I still have a sense of searing anger against my Biddulph grandparents, is evidence of the scar left upon my own mind.

In 1916, during the Great War, ten years after my parents' marriage, when my father was in the Army in France and I was a boy of eight

Shaen Magan, my father, as a First War Emergency officer

years of age, I one morning found my mother sitting bowed over a table weeping. I tried to comfort her, but she was inconsolably grieved, and continued to shake with her sobbing.

Had my father been killed? No; it was her own father who had died. She had loved him, but he had cast her out and never seen or spoken to her again. The sorrows and bereavements of might-have-beens are indeed more bitter, haunting and lasting than those that may follow the close of happy fulfilment.

How could Assheton Biddulph have been so obstinately cruel to her, his favourite daughter? How could he have been so lacking in human affection? She had been his constant companion for years in the hunting field, climbing the Slieve Bloom mountains and fishing the mountain streams. He was a Christian. Had he never heard of the Prodigal Son? That he had a quite unnaturally stony-hearted wife was no excuse. 'The woman gave me of the tree,' did not save Adam from the wrath of God. Nor will it absolve my maternal grandfather, Assheton Biddulph, from mine, or from my contempt. His wife, my maternal grandmother Florence Biddulph, I regard as wickedness personified. And she made a great mistake. My father would have been a most dutiful son-in-law. After her husband and her son died in the same year, my father would have given her all the help and advice she urgently needed in very difficult circumstances, during the Irish rebellion, in which she had to struggle to run Moneyguyneen and its home farm, and when country estates were being threatened, and country houses burnt, by the IRA. My father and my Aunt Violet did no less for Middleton Biddulph at great risk to themselves.

Chapter 3

My Beginning

My birth took place on 13 June 1908 in a house named 'The Cottage' on the estate of the Dames-Longworth family, Glynnwood, which lies to the east of Athlone, between the town and the Quaker town of Moate, in the county of Westmeath.

I was born there because my father had borrowed the house as the house he had rented on the outskirts of Athlone was not yet ready for occupation. After his father's death at the end of 1903, he had decided to leave the family home in Roscommon and move nearer to Athlone where his main business interests were centred.

At that time babies were customarily born in the home, not in hospital. My mother and I survived, and she also survived the birth of her other four children. As we were told at quite a young age that our Biddulph grandmother wished all my mother's children dead, we had that thought hanging over us since we were very young – a thought that was to have particular significance for me before I was much older.

My mother was twenty-seven years of age, and my father twenty-eight, at the time of my birth. They had been married two and a half years, and already had one other child, my older sister, Annie Sheelagh. There was, I was told, great satisfaction at the birth of a son and, as a spontaneous perpetuation of the recognition of that, I was known from then on, until a measure of relief came later, by the dreadful name of Sonny, despite having been given three immediately to be discarded Christian names – or forenames, as they are now called – William Morgan Tilson.

Not long after my birth, my parents moved to their new home,

Oldcourt. In money matters my father was a prudent man. Although he was well enough off to marry and lead a full and comfortable life, he was not rich. Not only had he known his own father to be extravagant, but he was also well aware that many other 'gentry' families in rural Ireland were living beyond their means, just to keep up appearances. So, despite the fact that his background was of a long line of rich Irish landowners, he was not himself tempted to risk insolvency by lavishing money on appearances; and he thus chose for himself a house of sensible size and appointments when he decided to rent Oldcourt. My mother, too, was a thrifty person and, although her father cut a great dash as MFH in the King's County, she too was totally devoid of any temptation to pretentious living.

Oldcourt was a Georgian house situated just beyond the north edge of Athlone. It was on the road which is now the T31 leading to Ballymahon, and it lay in the fork between two railways, the Great Southern and Western, usually known as the 'Southern', and the Midland Great Western, usually called the 'Midland', where they converged on Athlone. The house has now been pulled down to make way for a residential estate. The site and some of the outbuildings and walls were much older than the house itself.

The property was perhaps about six acres, including a walled garden and two small fields where we kept a couple of cows for milk for the household. The road ran along the east boundary of the little estate, and the outbuildings backed on to it. The entrance gates, with a curved wall at each side, were set back in a half-moon bay off the road at the south-east corner of the property – the part nearest the town. The wall by the gate was to become a very familiar perch for me.

The drive to the house – which faced west – was short. From it a flight of stone steps led up to the pillared portico entrance to the house, and the hall door leading into the central hall.

The accommodation corresponded to what was generally regarded in the nineteenth century as appropriate to the needs of a professional upper-class family – that of a clergyman, a doctor or a lawyer; and such as would be likely to be found on the outskirts of a thriving town like Athlone, in the neighbourhood of which there were a number of such houses – houses with three or four reception rooms, four to seven bedrooms, ample kitchen quarters, larder, pantry, dairy and so on; and accommodation for nurses, governesses, and up to three or four servants.

The indoor part of my earliest life was spent almost entirely in two of those rooms: the schoolroom, the commodious reception room in the north-west corner of the ground floor; and the nursery, the bedroom immediately above the schoolroom.

When I was eighteen months old, my next sister, Violet Mary, was born in December 1909. As in my case, her given names were ignored because both were already 'occupied'; Violet by her aunt, my father's youngest and favourite sister, and Mary by the cook; so, instead, she was called 'Tiny' – to give way in a few years to 'Mollie' as she was to be known for the rest of her life. Thus Sheelagh and Mollie and I became the inhabitants of the schoolroom and the bedroom above, in which we all slept. It was to be another five years before the next child, Maureen, was to be born. I have no recollection of our nurses, but, in 1911, there arrived an English nursery governess, aged perhaps in her late twenties. She, and we three children, shared the schoolroom for the next four years, and she slept in a small room next to our bedroom. Such were the formalities of the time that she was never called by her Christian name. I do not even know what it was. She was always 'Miss Hatton' to our parents and the staff.

My earliest personal memory goes back to a time when I was not yet three years old. I was taken to a Dublin nursing home and there an eminent surgeon, Sir Arthur Ball, performed upon me a hernia operation – right side. I remember being in bed and feeling very hot, very thirsty and very uncomfortable. I wanted, above everything, an apple, and for years afterwards I was mocked with imitations of my plaintive cries for one. Despite the intensive religious bombardment and indoctrination that I was already beginning to undergo, I did not yet know enough to throw a Bible quotation in their teeth: 'Stay me with flagons, and comfort me with apples.' The Bible has everything, even to knowing what you want after a hernia operation!

My mother kindly stayed in the nursing home with me, but I only dimly remember her being there. The nurses I do not recall at all; but

I have a dim and faded, but still sharply outlined, recollection of the room, and of Sir Arthur Ball coming through the door and standing by the bed and speaking, I think, kindly to me. I felt I had need of kindness.

It must have been shortly after that that Miss Hatton arrived. We called her 'Minnar'. She was a good woman, and a responsible and dutiful person. She had an even temper, and an even temperament. She did not have moods or get unduly cross. Indeed, I think she must have had great patience. But, correspondingly, I think she was somewhat lacking in sparkle. The life we lived intimately with her for years was safe and predictable, but perhaps duller than it might have been with someone more high-spirited and affectionate. Indeed, I look back on my earliest years as deadly boring. But how Miss Hatton herself stomached the tedium of her life with such uncomplaining resignation, is hard to imagine.

She was virtually imprisoned for four years in two rooms with three restless children; and although, as we grew older, we spent more and more time on our own out of doors, she still had to take us for a boring daily walk. When we grew too old for a nursery governess, she left us, and spent the whole of the rest of her life doing the same thing over and over again with other people's children. She should be canonised. She brought us up – and many others – as good children, with decent ideas.

We loved Minnar dearly. Young children, however self-centred they may seem, are at the same time full of a natural affection which, like dogs, they must lavish on someone. We lavished ours on Miss Hatton and on our mother, but we saw much less of our mother, so Miss Hatton got the lion's share. She might, and often did, dutifully no doubt, correct us with the hairbrush, the ruler or the strap, as was the custom at that time, but again, like dogs, we were prepared to accept that from someone we loved, without letting it impair our affection.

Indeed, the strap, the hairbrush and the ruler became hardly more than symbolic between us. They were never used to excess or brutally, and were so much a part of the normal course of our lives that Mollie and I used to wallop each other by agreement just to keep in training.

Miss Hatton was good to us, as countless governesses were good to other children, but the affection we received was on the chilly side, as was that received by other governessed children. We were denied the spontaneous loving warmth to which we would have responded in full measure. This, perhaps, more than anything else, accounts for the supposedly traditional reserve of the upper-class English. Their responses were deliberately repressed in their earliest years. We were not warmly hugged or kissed. Children need to caress and to be caressed. We were not even touched, other than with the hairbrush or the strap, or to have our faces and hands rubbed with a wet flannel, and I am sure that any attempt to caress Miss Hatton would have been resisted by her.

Chapter 4

Indoors - Daytime

Indoors and out-of-doors were two different worlds in our very early life. I shall therefore deal with them in separate chapters; though I shall not draw too rigid a distinction between them. Indoors was real life. Out-of-doors was exceptional, requiring special measures – changes of footwear and clothing, accompaniment by grown-ups, or special permission as to the scope and nature of any outdoor venture.

The day started with washing and dressing in the bedroom, where there was no running water, but an old-fashioned china wash-basin filled from a china jug of cold water which was kept full in the bedroom. Hot water was brought to the bedroom in a brass jug by one of the maids. I can still feel, and smell, the awful sensation of having my face rubbed, and my nose squashed, with a damp flannel.

The bedroom was cold, and in winter we shivered into our clothes. There was no gas or electricity. Heating was from open fires, and we sometimes had a fire in the evening in the bedroom, but not in the early morning. Lighting was candles and oil lamps.

Breakfast was at 8.30 a.m., and was in the schoolroom where we had all our meals. Our parents ate in the dining-room, but we never had meals with them. There was always porridge for breakfast; always, always. It was not, I think, until a decade or so later, that the sort of cereals we have today became common in Britain and Ireland, when most households began to use an early cornflake named 'Force'.

Either our porridge was of poor quality - my mother's thrift - or it was badly cooked. It usually had lumps in it which were quite disgusting, but we had to eat it, lumps and all. Sometimes it was

33

burnt. That was awful. But whatever its condition, *we had to eat it*. No
backsliding.

What followed was better, eggs and bacon perhaps or, what I liked
best, soft-boiled eggs into which we were allowed to dip fingers of
bread and butter. Never toast. It was a luxury, and not allowed.
Luxuries were unchristian, and bad for the character.

To finish, there was bread and butter, or bread and jam – perhaps
marmalade. Bread and butter and jam together were not allowed on
two counts: extravagance and luxury. Butter must not be thickly
spread. We called it 'bread and scrape'.

Bread must be home-made soda bread, white or brown, and several
days old and rather stale. Fresh bread was luxurious and bad for the
digestion as well as for the character. 'Baker's bread' was allowed only
as a rare treat; and lovely fresh baker's bread as a blue moon treat –
unhealthy, indigestible, luxurious, unchristian.

Perhaps this was good upbringing. It had a benefit which I think
children do not have today. 'Treats' really were treats. A piece of toast
– made with a toasting fork in front of the fire: there were no electric
toasters – was a mouth-watering treat, as were many other quite
ordinary things, such as sweet biscuits. Are there any treats for
children today, or do they have it all as a matter of course?

One treat was when the jampot was empty. We were allowed to
pour some milk into it and mix it with the remnants of the jam and
drink it.

It was cold in the schoolroom at that hour of the morning. There
were no all-night burning stoves, not even in the kitchen. The kitchen
'range', as the large black cooking stove was known, went out at night
and had to be cleaned out very early in the morning by one of the
maids, re-laid with paper, kindling wood and a few well chosen pieces
of coal, and re-lit. Laying and lighting fires was an art. One man,
Johnnie Lane, who had worked for my grandfather in Roscommon,
told me that as a boy he had had the job in winter of laying and
lighting fourteen fires in the house every morning. There were no fire
lighters in those days.

The schoolroom had an open grate on which coal, or rather
'slack', was burnt. It, too, had to be cleaned out and lit before we

came down to breakfast.

Slack was coal dust and small coal fragments, damped with water till it became a sort of viscous paste which lay in the fire-place in a lump. In that condition, when lit, it smouldered very slowly until all the damp had dried out, when it could be coaxed into flame. However, in my mother's view, it was unchristian and uneconomical to have a flaming fire before four o'clock in the afternoon. Until then, the slack steamed gently and must not be poked or disturbed. But come four o'clock, we could thrust a poker through the centre of the hard slack crust, and we would then be rewarded with a splendid thick upward-spiralling column of bluey-yellow smoke, to be followed shortly by a flicker or two of flames. Eventually, we would have the enjoyment for the rest of the evening of a fire, with the addition of some lumps of coal, a few logs, and some 'sods of turf', as peat is called in Ireland. Was this bad or good? Was there not perhaps some merit in having something to look forward to in the evening, after half-shivering our way through the day? Almost life's greatest boon is having something to which to look forward. Nevertheless, nearly all children in those days suffered from appalling and painful chilblains. No-one seems to get them now. There was no domestic central heating.

The mornings were for lessons. I did not mind them. Those at which I was good, I positively enjoyed. From Miss Hatton I learnt to read and write. I read aloud, and was, and have always remained, a slow reader.

Writing was in printed 'exercise books'. The earliest were 'pot-hooks and hangers' - curved shapes like the hooks and hangers used even then to hang pots over open fires. Each row of pot-hooks and hangers in the exercise book was followed by a blank row in which, with a pencil, I had to try to copy the row above. When we had mastered the pot-hooks and hangers, we graduated to exercise books of single letters of the alphabet to be copied. Then books of words; then sentences - 'The cat sat on the mat'. The earliest example of my handwriting that survives is when I was just six years old.

We learnt the alphabet by heart in the old form. It has been of inestimable use. Can you look up 'ker' or 'ger' in a dictionary? I don't know. I can, however, look up 'c' or 'g'.

Miss Hatton taught me elementary mathematics. Arithmetic, I particularly enjoyed. Another accomplishment of life-long use was my 'tables' up to twelve times. I was good and quick at mental arithmetic – addition, subtraction, multiplication, division. All, together with long-division, have been a valuable part of life's baggage. Thank you Minnar, and also for teaching me algebra and elementary geometry.

History, I greatly enjoyed. English I do not remember, except 'dictation', though I must have learnt grammar and spelling, but I have remained a bad speller all my life. I think spelling is physiological. There is some group of cells in the brain that either does or does not work efficiently. The good speller can't make a mistake. To do so would be as obvious, and as painful, as it would be to someone with perfect pitch to sing flat. The bad speller is no less – to continue the metaphor – naturally the equivalent of tone deaf. However hard he tries, he cannot altogether learn the trick. He cannot summon up the spelling equivalent of perfect pitch, and he can sing flat – i.e. make a spelling mistake – without being aware of it. But dictation I enjoyed, even if I spelt the words wrongly. I had an excellent memory, and could write long passages of dictation word for word perfect.

I think scripture completed my curriculum. I shall come to it in another context.

Unfortunately, Miss Hatton taught me no Latin or French. That was a handicap when I went to school, and I never really surmounted it.

I was unlucky to miss becoming perhaps nearly bilingual in German and English. That came about because my mother, who had learnt some German when studying music in Dresden, added to the household, in the summer of 1914, a young German governess. I liked her very much; she had a younger, warmer and much less starched personality than Miss Hatton, and I am sure I would have got on like a house on fire at learning German with her. But on 4 August 1914, the United Kingdom, of which the whole of Ireland was then a part, found itself at war with Germany, and my new-found German friend had, to my great sorrow, to go home. I was altogether

Sheelagh and I with Miss Hatton, the nursery governess, c1912

puzzled by this development, and asked my mother. 'Do I now have to hate her?' If so, I knew it was a patriotic duty in which I could not prove to be other than a hopeless failure. I was at least slightly in love with her.

Morning lessons were followed by lunch in the schoolroom. Perhaps I remember only the worst of it, but my mother did have a reputation for giving her children dull fare. She was motivated by three things. First, what was good for our souls. We must not be spoilt. We must not be pampered, or allowed to be soft. We must be stoical and accustomed to hard tack. Secondly, plain, honest fare was, she believed, more healthy and better for us than dressed up foods. Thirdly, thrift. No more than necessary must be spent on food, or fuel, or any other creature comforts.

Let me hasten to repeat, lest I give an unfair impression - and before I recall some of the menus - that my mother was a sweet and simple woman, and that we loved her dearly, as did everyone else; but she was tenaciously immoveable in her black and white views on what was right and wrong, what was good or bad.

I will be brief about the lunchtime menus in the Oldcourt schoolroom, because mercifully my memory of them is not too strong. Boiled cod was a frequent dish. It came in a solid lump, wrapped in black skin like the bitumenised paper wrapping of bicycle tyres. It was swimming in a gravy of salt and boiling water, and was accompanied by a glutinous white sauce peppered with small pieces of chopped up hard-boiled egg. With it were served very dry potatoes boiled in their skins - always boiled, and always in their jackets. We did not have to eat the skins. How we longed for the season of new potatoes. And there was a vegetable: the worst horrors were white turnips and parsnips - always boiled. I cannot think why I still have some liking for cabbage and mashed mangelwurzels.

Two other stalwarts of the lunchtime menu in the Oldcourt schoolroom were boiled sheep's head and boiled calf's head, grinning scavengings from Golgotha which came whole on a dish swimming in the familiar salt and boiling water gravy. When, at an early age, my scripture lessons brought me to the story of Salome, it was no novelty for me. I knew just what 'a head on a charger' was like.

At all events, from these macabre dishes lumps of meat were plucked which we ate *faute de mieux* without any relish. Tripe was another of my mother's delicacies which I enjoyed, and a welcome occasional dish was brawn.

Irish country cooking was virtually limited to boiling in iron pots – I got a wigging from a learned reviewer for not calling the pots 'trivets' in my last book; but did any Irish cottager ever call them trivets? I never heard the word in rural Ireland. The reviewer, too, was in error. A trivet is not a pot. It is a stand on which pots are stood in the hearth. Never mind; the iron pots were hung over the open fires in the enormous cottage hearths, or were stood in the hot turf embers. This exclusive boiling may have been much more healthy than, for instance, frying. Irish country people were certainly very healthy. A natural outcome was, I suppose, that those women who became cooks in the larger houses brought with them a preference for – and a skill in – boiling, which influenced the menus in their new surroundings.

We did sometimes get more interesting dishes. On Sundays, there was roast mutton or roast beef which, at the end of the week, could become mince or rissoles, which we enjoyed. One of my sisters said that the weekly regime was 'hot meat, cold meat and old meat'. Boiled bacon and cabbage and mashed potato was another favourite, as was colcannon, a sort of mince of potato, bacon and cabbage. Bubble and squeak made a welcome change of vegetable.

Puddings were no less plain. There was invariably a milk pudding: revolting gelatinous tapioca, which we called 'frog-spawn', and its no more amiable first cousin, sago. There was usually a fruit dish with the milk pudding: prunes, for instance. Apple was sometimes cooked into the tapioca; it was very agreeable and was called by my mother Tappi-appi. One very common combination in the spring months was always greeted by an intoned chorus, like a chant, as it was brought through the door by the maid – 'Rhuuubarb – and – Riiiice!'

There were other puddings. 'Shape' – blancmange – was usually white, flavoured with vanilla; rarely chocolate; sometimes variegated, streaked with cochineal. Then there were steamed puddings – jam roly-poly, spotted dog, treacle pudding, and – the best of them –

marmalade pudding. Occasionally there was treacle tart, but that was getting onto dangerous ground: verging on the luxurious.

Whether this sort of culinary regime was good or bad for us, I don't know. Curiously, however, I have retained a preference all my life for plain food, and boiled food at that.

There was grace before and after meals. So: 'For what we are about to receive, the Lord make us truly thankful'; and afterwards, 'Thank God for my good lunch [or whatever]; please may I get down.'

After lunch we went for a walk, and after that it was back to the schoolroom. There were no lessons in the afternoon. We played with our toys. I had a toy fort and lead soldiers and fought endless battles. Sometimes, when we got older, we played board games – snakes and ladders, Ludo, draughts which I loved, and other such games as dominoes, spillikins and tiddly-winks, and various card games.

Or Miss Hatton would read to us – all the fairy tales when we were very young: Grimms', Hans Andersen's, and I forget what else; and, when we got older, *Black Beauty*, over which we wept buckets, *Little Lord Fauntleroy*, and no doubt all the other nursery favourites. I marvel that that good woman could have read our favourites over and over again without expiring of boredom. How many times did I implore her to read 'Tom Thumb', my favourite fairytale?

Perhaps, because we three children were very much of an age, and therefore, no doubt, always disturbing each other's concentration, and perhaps, too, because Miss Hatton read so much to us, I did not, I think, develop a very strong personal reading habit during my childhood, though I was to catch up in the next phase, in my boyhood.

My sisters were encouraged to learn to sew and knit and crochet, and my mother played a large part in this instruction. This was treated not as lessons, but as fun. My mother was a good needlewoman, a magnificent, tireless and voluminous knitter, and could crochet like the best of them, if need be. I also learnt a little sewing, knitting and crocheting. I was not pressed very hard with my endeavours, because these were not deemed manly pursuits. I can sew on a button. That is about all. My knitting was largely a stitch-dropping fumble; but I have to my credit a few pairs of crocheted woollen garters.

Unfortunately I did little or nothing with my hands. There were no plastic construction games like Lego. Such plastic sophistications were half a century away. There were wooden bricks, but they required little skill, dexterity, imagination or ingenuity. I had some Meccano – perforated metal in different shapes and sizes. It could be bolted together to make various facsimile objects, but it was a tedious job, and really rather beyond the possible skill of small children. My father was no handyman, and neither my mother nor Miss Hatton were skilled with tools.

When I was a little older, someone was good enough, and imaginative enough, to give me a small microscope. This was right up Miss Hatton's street, and she helped me to use it. We had great fun and interest examining spiders' legs, segments of butterflies' wings, and other scarcely visible parts of plants and insects. But it did not turn me into a scientist.

There were no electric toys, but I had some clockwork ones. My favourite was a small railway set. Children like toys that move under their own motive power – an ancient primitive cat and mouse instinct perhaps.

At five o'clock in the afternoon came tea. We could drink water or milk. Drinks like squashes and today's 'fizzy' drinks were rare – generally so, I think, and certainly in our house where they were unknown to us. Indeed, I recall that when, sometime much later, we were given some fizzy lemonade, we said we liked the lemon, but we didn't like the 'ade'.

To eat, there was the stalish bread and 'scrape'. After that, home-made jam. That was all there was for tea except sometimes barm brack – a delicious baker-made loaf, loaded with currants and a little spice, and eaten with butter. But that was a treat.

On Sundays there was cake – a very dry home-made cake rather sparsely dotted with fruit. In later life it came to be called 'missionary cake', until later still it was superseded by an excellent fruit cake known as 'the Colonel's Cake', because my father particularly enjoyed it, he having acquired that rank in World War I. On Sundays, too, there might be biscuits, but rather dull ones. After tea, my mother would often join us. There were two games that my mother particularly liked – tiddly-winks and spillikins. They were good games since both required a little manual dexterity.

This very restricted regime relaxed itself as we grew older. Three-, four- and five-year-olds may perhaps be confined more or less to one room. Older than that, they need more scope, and we began to have greater use of the house generally. We could not be imprisoned all the time, and Miss Hatton could not live the life of an unrelieved gaoler. We could sometimes spend time in the kitchen with the servants. Curiously, I have no precise memory of any of the servants of my earliest years, or of their names. They always wore uniform – black dresses with white aprons and white lace caps. The cook had a different, and more functional, uniform, and was less elegant than the maids. The servants were kind and friendly, and we could give a hand with pots and pans and mixing and so on, and that was all very agreeable. And sometimes we could join in something that might be going on. For instance, I recall a happy morning helping my mother to unpack a packing-case of stores that had come from some Dublin shop. Thus, as we grew older and more independent, and gained more freedom and more scope, life became much less boring.

Miss Hatton was interested in photography. There was no coloured photography; the industry was in its infancy and cameras were very primitive. But she had a Box Brownie-Two camera taking pictures of 2½ x 3½ inches, and she developed the negatives herself and made her own prints. Prints could be either matte or glossy, grey or sepia. That was all very interesting and exciting. I preferred matte sepia prints. Mollie and I developed an interest in photography, and I did some developing and printing. I never became an expert, but I have in consequence taken photos all my life. For such interest and pleasure as I have had in photography, I have Miss Hatton to thank.

There was a piano in the drawing-room, but Miss Hatton did not play, and we did not have regular lessons. Nevertheless, I did learn to read the notes and to play a little, probably from my mother. She was not a pianist, but she was a good violinist and a musical person, though becoming even then less and less able to enjoy it because of an increasing chronic deafness. Her deafness was a disgrace and should never have happened. Aged sixteen, at school in England, towards the end of an Easter term, she had developed measles. Her father insisted on having her home to attend the hunt ball before she had fully recuperated; the consequence was a lifetime of chronic deafness, about which she was too good ever to complain.

I cannot imagine where I learnt all the tunes that were in my head. All the old music hall songs and popular light operatic music of the time, are familiar to me. Perhaps people were always singing, humming or whistling them. Gramophones, hand wound, as electric motors were not then used in them, were rare, and we did not have one; and the later portable variety was still ten years away. Wireless telegraphy had lately been invented, but radio programmes for general home consumption were still more than twenty years away. Television was not to come for another forty years.

There was a comparable lack of automatic household appliances: no refrigerators; no clothes-washing and drying machines; no dish-washing machines; no electric mixing machines; no automatic kitchen gadgets, no vacuum cleaners; no immersion heaters for hot water; no electric fires or central heating; no electric switches because there was no electricity. Everything had to be done by hand, and there had to be such ingenious contrivances as people could make to keep things hot or cool.

This century, the twentieth century, has been the century of oil. Oil was being exploited in North America in the latter part of the nineteenth century, but it was not until 1901 that the first Middle East oil concession was obtained by Britain. Since then oil has placed at the disposal of human society an increase of energy such as had never been known in the world before. It is that that has enabled the enormous scientific developments of this century. It is to that that we can give thanks for our abundant electricity today with all the ingenious gadgets which it makes possible, and for the liberty that motor cars and aircraft have given us; also for the wealth that has enabled the research that has done so much to improve health care; and for many other blessings. But we should not overlook the fact that the abundance of oil and the wealth it has created have also given rise to, or enabled, some very dangerous and undesirable developments.

Common in the kitchens of those days was enamel-ware, chiefly plates and mugs, and never, I think, seen today, though I still have one enamel mug which did many years' duty as a shaving mug.

Miss Hatton had a half-day a week off, perhaps Wednesday or Thursday afternoon, and that was all. Our mother then looked after us, and took us for our walk, and gave us tea. We enjoyed that. We could take more liberties with her. She never condescended to us. She was more of a grown-up friend. But there was no relaxation of the austerities over the fire; or over the half-stale bread, butter and jam character of the tea. And no hugs or cuddles at that time of day. We were not to be brought up soft.

Chapter 5

Indoors – Night-time

B edtime, doubtless, got progessively later as we grew older, but when we were very young it was probably half-past six, and later on perhaps half-past seven, but I think not much later as there had to be time for the grown-ups to get ready for dinner at eight. Meals were held punctually at set times, otherwise the servants, and particularly the cook, could not organise their day.

In the winter, going up to bed meant going by candlelight. It was something you did not do alone. We knew all about ghosts and spooks and witches, and giants too; and a shakily held flickering candle on dark stairs or in the board-creaking blackness of a terrifying tunnel of a passage, could cast moving spectral shadows that would turn your flesh cold and stand the hair on the back of your neck on end. So, to give ourselves courage, we went noisily up the stairs in a body, clutching the grown-ups' hands.

I was given an electric 'flashlight', as torches were then called, when I was about five years old. It was rectangular in shape like a cigarette packet. It had a sliding top allowing a variety of three colours when switched on – white, green or red. One day, when I was trying to put the top back after changing the battery, it slipped and gave me a deep cut at the base of my right thumb. I have the scar to this day. I was told cheerfully at the time that I would probably get lockjaw – tetanus.

When we were very young, my mother helped to see us into bed. We enjoyed that. She hugged us, and blew down the back of our necks, and made us laugh. There was a fire in the bedroom in winter, and we were bathed in front of it in a flat, round bath, painted brown on the outside and white on the inside. It rested on a large bath mat, six times the size of any bath mat you would see today. On the floor in front of the fire were jugs or cans of hot and cold water, brought there by the maids, and the bath was filled from them to the desired temperature. There was a bathroom in the house, a luxury which by no means all houses had, but we did not use it until we were older.

After the bath and teeth washing, there was some romping and playing, and perhaps story-telling, until it was time to get into bed. But there was one last duty of the day – prayers.

Our prayers were of a kind conventional to the nursery. We each knelt by our bed and said our prayers aloud. They started with 'God bless . . .' followed by a nominal roll of near members of the family. I don't think the servants were included, or Miss Hatton. A favourite animal might get squeezed in now and again, or a servant for a special favour rendered – a surreptitious titbit passed across *sub rosa* in the kitchen, perhaps.

Then we had one or two little children's prayers. My favourite, for it both conjured up spectacular and comprehensible images and offered the possibility of doing some good, was a hymn verse:

> Grant to little children,
> Visions bright of thee;
> [That didn't excite me. It was simply a word version of the
> common pictures of Our Lord with a halo.]
> Guard the sailors tossing
> On the deep blue sea.

That was a very different matter. In my mental image, the sea wasn't very blue. It was ink black, wild and stormy, with low, dark, wind-torn rags of cloud racing across the moon. The sailors were in an open boat, with oars. The boat was standing almost on end as it rode up a huge creaming wave with angry spray and spindrift whipped off the top by the gale. Imagination carried the scene no further. It must have had its origin in some picture book. The boat and the sailors were in the same predicament every night, and were clearly worth praying for, and I prayed for them like mad.

My prayers ended, less fervently, less hopefully and less wishfully, perhaps, with: 'And please make me a good boy.'

A little later on in life, when we were still very young, we were taught the Lord's Prayer. The first line, 'Our Father who art in Heaven,' conjured up a certain image. The rest was just words, except the 'daily bread' which seemed a curiously unappetising thing for which to pray. Because learning by heart was so easy to me, there was no problem with the words, but I am afraid the Lord's Prayer just became a meaningless racing gabble and to be told, 'Slower, slower,' proved an ineffectual brake on my performance. That it achieved its object, to benefit me spiritually no doubt, must remain highly questionable.

When we were in bed, and kissed by my mother – Miss Hatton did not kiss us – and bidden, 'Goodnight, sleep tight,' and all that, the grown-ups withdrew. A nightlight was left burning, and in winter I loved the shadows on the ceiling of the last flickers of the fire as one dying coal after another flared up and expired. Occasionally we had a dreg or two of energy left and, instead of falling immediately to sleep, had a final burst of activity. A favourite adventure was to tie a sheet over the top of Mollie's cot, which had high sides and ends, and make a tent. I recall no severe consequences of these adventures.

In the summer, I think I was more wakeful. Since our room faced west, the sun still shone when we were supposed to be going to sleep, and I envied the freedom of the blackbirds singing their heads off outside. But there was one occurrence which happened every night, soon after 'lights-out', which had a terrifying fascination for me.

A mile or so to the west of where we lived was the wide Shannon river. Just the far side of it was the 'Midland' railway station. Soon after our lights out was the time for the evening passenger express to leave for Dublin along the line which was the boundary of one of our fields. All trains were steam trains then, and I knew when the express began to pull out of the station, because I could hear the first few great chuffs as the steam was injected by the driver through the majestic cylinders. Also, as the engine took the first strain, the driving wheels often spun, greatly increasing the noise and its frequency. 'Chuff . . . chuff . . . chuff . . .' it would start, with long intervals between the chuffs; and then chuff, chuff, chuff, chuff, chuff, chuff, chuff, very quickly as the wheels spun. Then the steady haul would begin with gradually decreasing intervals between the chuffs as the heavy train gathered way.

Immediately after leaving the station, the train crossed the Shannon railway bridge. The bridge must have had a deck of wooden sleepers, because there was a deep hollow rumble as the train rolled across it.

Then the express was out in the open, gathering speed and coming towards me. Nearer and nearer it came with more and more noise. Then it was roaring past our field belching steam and smoke.

I believe I am not a romantic person, but who could not be moved by the romance of a tearing steam passenger express, wreathed in smoke and vapour, the very embodiment of plutonic force and violence, the fire box glowing, the fireman, a veritable salamander, shovelling coal into it for his life; the noble figure of the engine driver with one hand on the controls, the other clutching a fistful of cotton waste, looking ahead watchfully through the forward window of his cab.

But these wonders were not my concern at that awesome moment when the train roared past. I never saw that train. I dared not look; because it carried a terrifying cargo. The guard's van was full of witches and, as it rushed past our field, the doors opened and out they flew. Black cloaks flying; tall Welsh hats askew; mounted on their broomsticks, through the swirling smoke and steam, and the din and racket of the train they came, streaking across the field, skinny, bony, gnarled fingers crooked to get me. I was firmly under the bedclothes, gathering them tightly around me, and I did not come out till the last rumble of the accelerating express had died away into the distance. I suppose the idea derived from a threat by some nursemaid that if I was not good a witch would come after me.

Trains in the daytime I enjoyed. They were not infected, or infested, with witches. Only that one.

I shared the disturbing nightly reveries of the ghostly witches and the imperilled sailors with no-one. They were my own private fantasies, my personal terrors and anxieties. Do children need some such disquieting - even frightening - fancies, or visions, to stimulate and exercise those warning faculties of vigilance common to wild animals and birds? They are part of their defence and security mechanisms, and are no doubt implanted in us humans too, but, in our more secure, artificial human conditions, are they in danger of becoming rusty and blunted by disuse?

A marvellous occasional summer bedtime experience would be a thunderstorm. I loved thunderstorms then and have loved them ever since. How could anyone do other than watch and listen when forty thousand feet of Indian monsoon cumulo-nimbus cloud is giving an incomparable display of lightning, and crashing, echoing, rumbling and muttering thunder, with rain coming down in stair rods at two or three inches an hour, and bouncing two feet off the ground? Or, in the Himalayas, three or four storms at the same time, putting on an unimaginable show of pyrotechnics, with every thunderclap echoing a dozen times through the hills and valleys.

Our nursery thunderstorms were not of that order, though sometimes awesome enough. We were not frightened by them. We knew what they were. They were giants playing football with thunderbolts. Giants were frightening, but so long as they went on playing football with the clouds between them and us, we were safe. So thunderstorms were not only exciting things, but also good things since they kept giants safely busy.

One more 'after lights out' experience in which I revelled was the winter gales. It thrilled me to hear the shake and roar of the strongest gusts in the chimney, and the rain lashing with stinging fury on the window panes. Snug in my bed, I sensed the primeval satisfaction of the warm security of a dry lair, and so would fall asleep.

We acknowledged some of the landmarks in the calendar. We were conscious that New Year's Day was special, but were too young to usher it in. On the 1st April, we tried to make April fools of each other. Easter we celebrated with eggs, real and chocolate, and cotton-wool yellow chickens. Midsummer's Day passed unnoticed. But we roasted chestnuts and ate apples on Halloween - a bad time for me with the air full of witches. We were aware of Guy Fawkes day but I do not remember bonfires or fireworks. It would not have been like my father to burn money in the shape of a few squibs.

Sheelagh, myself and Mollie

Christmas Day was excitingly ushered in - no doubt too early - with stockings hanging on our bed-ends, full and fat, with this and that but I forget what, except the perennial orange; and there was Christmas fare, turkey and plum-pudding, crackers and Christmas cake, paper hats, whistles and so on. And, for New Year fare, there was always a goose.

The fantasy of the witches in the guard's van of trains suggests that something should be said about railway travel in those days. It was the normal way of undertaking any journey of any distance. The few who had motor cars might have gone distances of twenty or thirty miles but probably for any journey beyond that they would have taken a railway train. My father would never have thought of going from Athlone to Dublin - eighty miles - by car.

Trains had 1st, 2nd and 3rd class. 2nd class dropped out early in my life and we were left with 1st and 3rd. There were no open-plan coaches - only compartments in which there was no heating. It was possible in winter to hire metal canisters of hot water as foot warmers. As children we travelled 3rd class - not very comfortable.

Because of all the smoke and soot belched out by the engine, the trains could not be very clean, and an open window on a hot day was likely to let in more dirt.

For all that, trains did greatly facilitate movement, and added enormously to the distance that could be travelled in a limited time in what was still a largely horse-drawn age.

Chapter 6

Outdoors - the Precincts

Outdoors had three dimensions. Just being outside was one general and different dimension from indoors. More light, wind, breeze, moving air, weather, mist, rain, drizzle, sunshine; temperature changes; at times even frost and snow; all of them providing sensations acutely distinguishing outdoors from indoors in the highly receptive state of childhood perception.

The other two dimensions were the two worlds: one within the boundaries of our own domain; the other, the wider world beyond.

The precincts, as I have headed this chapter, comprised the first of those worlds, the world within our own home boundaries. It consisted, in addition to the house itself, of a number of distinct entities.

There was the stable yard with coach house, stables, cow house, pigsty, hen houses, wood store, and coal hole, and perhaps other offices - a hay loft no doubt. There were no garages in those days; we had no motor car. They were very rare.

There was the walled garden, with both flowers and vegetables, and the lawn in front of the house, with a noble lime tree in the middle with a seat around its base. Beyond were two fields with trees in them and along some of the verges, and there was a shrubbery leading down the avenue to the entrance gate and its flanking walls, one of which was to become so important to me.

That, for those days, was not living on a grand scale, but it was a big enough world for us in early childhood.

In the stable block and outhouses interesting things happened. My mother kept horses and hunted, but these 'grown-up' horses were remote from us. Of more interest were a donkey and a pony which, being black, or dark brown, was inevitably called Black Beauty.

My dear mother was highly unimaginative. As the daughter of a famous MFH, she wanted her children to be good horsemen and women. At the earliest possible age, therefore, we were put to ride the donkey. Part of the initiation theory was that if you could ride bareback for a start, you could ride anything. Saddles at that age were for softies, not for us.

So, with brief shorts, and in effect bare legs almost up to my bottom, I was put on that beastly donkey's bare, hairy back, and jogged about on it to my acute discomfort. A donkey has a backbone like a jagged razor, and a pelt – to a bare-legged child – like the quills of a porcupine. If I could sit well back on the donkey's pelvis there was more comfort, but gravity soon slipped me down onto the jagged

My mother with the children, Sheelagh, myself and Mollie, and Black Beauty

nobbles of the creature's spine. In so far as it might be possible for an infant to do so, I swore to remain a life-long pedestrian.

Black Beauty seemed to be the almost exclusive possession of my older sister Sheelagh, though why she was so favoured I know not. But then, calamity of calamities! Black Beauty took sick. There were daily, and then hourly, bulletins. The stable became a sort of intensive care unit – vets and people coming and going; head shakings and gloom. A pall of bleak and anxious anticipation hung over us all, and over our little world. Our prayers for the poor, dumb, equine invalid were fervent and intense, but all to no avail. The unfortunate Black Beauty expired; and we howled.

And then the obsequies: they are graven on my mind as though of yesterday. Why I do not know, but we were allowed to watch. A horse and cart did duty for hearse, and was drawn up outside the stable door. Men with ropes went into the dark and deathly interior. In a few minutes they came backing out again, the pathetic corpse of Black Beauty slung between them, belly up and hoofs in the air.

They lifted her into the make-shift hearse. Her cousin between the shafts moved off, and the last we saw of Black Beauty was her lifeless limbs wobbling and swaying to the movement of the cart as it turned out of the yard and out of sight for ever. Fortunately we did not ask, 'What next?' For doubtless it was the kennels – hounds need lots of meat. That is the first encounter that I recall with the death of an intimate.

Other things, some more pleasant, and some less pleasant, went on in the yard. The most pleasant was the hens. I had, I was told, 'good hands', and was careful; so, from a very early age, I was allowed to collect the eggs. Surely one of the most pleasurable tasks in the experience of mankind is collecting deliciously warm, clean hens' eggs from nesting boxes. After collection, the hay- or straw-strewn boxes are empty. Then next morning, miracle of miracles, each once more contains one, two, three, perhaps four, beautiful new eggs. I had one sorrow only about our eggs. Our hens were Black Minorcas; they are excellent layers, but their eggs are pure white. Brown eggs are nicer to gather, as I learnt when, from time to time, I had a chance to collect other people's hens' eggs.

The pigs I loved, especially the little ones if a sow had a litter. It was impressed upon me that it is insulting to pigs to call them dirty. Only humans make them dirty by forcing them to live in foul conditions. Our pigs were never dirty. They had fresh, clean straw, and were pink and clean themselves, and they grunted a greeting whenever we looked over the half door of their sty. It is said that cats look down upon us; dogs look up to us; but pigs look upon us as equals.

But the pigs weren't there for pleasure, either ours or theirs. They were the days when home-cured bacon - largely spoilt, too, by being too salty, because it was preserved in large barrels of brine - was a normal part of the diet of households living a country life.

And so the day would dawn when the poor pigs were due to suffer the fate implicit in the cycle of omnivorous man's domestication of edible animals. We were never allowed to watch, and I am sure did not want to, but our hearts stood still at the blood-curdling shrieks and yells of the pigs. It was before the days of 'humane killers', but no doubt the killing was swiftly and expertly done. Pigs do not like being pushed around, and the yelling was, doubtless, mainly in protest at being pushed and dragged to the place of slaughter.

The walled garden was a pleasant place. In it we each had our own little patch of garden in which we were encouraged to grow things, an experience which gave me what real gardeners regard as an unfortunate but inalienable, genuine, and warm, affection for London pride, mignonette, pansies and nasturtiums. What a rewarding plant the nasturtium is! Nothing deters it. It grows in great profusion, spreads all over the place, and flowers for ages with a beautiful large flower, and it is edible. Real gardeners turn up their noses at it, but it is a plant for ordinary mortals who appreciate any living thing that is bursting with unstinted generosity. My favourite scents among the flowers were wallflowers and roses.

The garden had a wrought iron gate, very tempting to climb, but, tree climbing being a favourite pastime with me, I was severely warned, time and again, against climbing that gate. It had a row of iron spikes along the top, and there was frequently recounted to me the grizzly tale of the boy who - disobedient like all boys - one day, against all orders and when no-one was looking, climbed just such a gate, slipped as he was going over the top, fell, and was impaled by a spike through his stomach. The warning was dreadful enough to deter me from yielding to the temptation. I used to consider it, and to practice impaling myself by pushing sticks into my stomach, but even that was enough to persuade me that impalement was not worth the risk. It gave me a very queasy feeling even to contemplate it.

The lawn in front of the house was not large and was divided from the field beyond by a wooden paling. That field and the second field were open to each other, and the horses, cows, pony and donkey grazed there together.

The great joy of the fields to me were buttercups and cowslips. Children are near the ground and very conscious of the wonder and beauty of wild plants. Cowslips are one of the loveliest and most endearing of wild flowers, but where have they gone? I seldom see them now. Have modern herbicides destroyed them?

Beyond the fields ran the railway line. There were very few trains, but they were a source of interest that never palled or waned.

Myself at Oldcourt, Athlone, 1914

In the summer, rugs would be spread on the lawn under the lime tree and we would have tea there, and there still rings in my ears the buzz of thousands of bees working the lime flowers.

Although there were no vacuum cleaners in those days, carpets had nevertheless to be cleaned. Wall to wall fitted carpets were not general, perhaps were unknown. The daily cleaning of the carpets was with a carpet-sweeper, known as a Bissel, but that was not considered enough. So once a year, I suppose in the spring, the heavy, loose fitting, rectangular carpets were lugged out onto the lawn, turned face down, and beaten all over the back with canes. I used to take a hand, and can still smell the clouds of choking dust that came out of the carpets with every whack of the cane.

As we grew older, we were free to wander at will throughout the property, and there was always plenty to do and plenty to interest us. This brings me in particular to the road gate. My normal way there was not down the avenue, but the more mysterious way, through the shrubbery.

The road beyond the gate was quite narrow. There was no tarmac then, nor any concrete roads, and our road was the usual construction of rolled stone chips. In the summer, if it was dry, it was dusty, with a whitish grey dust. In winter it was muddy, with its potholes full of water. There was very little traffic. Motor cars were very rare. If one a day passed along the road, that was probably about the limit. There were horse-drawn carts and vans, and an occasional smart trap. The riding horse had largely given way to the bicycle. Many people walked, and the commonest vehicle of all was the 'ass-cart' – a small unsprung rattling cart with a flat board for a seat and rope for reins, drawn by a donkey; excessively uncomfortable, and with no shelter against the weather, but it was every cottage woman's conveyance to market.

There were, of course, no cattle or sheep trucks. The motorised lorry had hardly been invented. Animals moved on the hoof, and large herds of cattle and flocks of sheep would come jostling and padding down the road. The odd pig or calf going to market, and of course fowl, would be stuffed into the back of the ass-cart.

From my vantage point on the wall by the gate, I could watch this passing scene. Sometimes there would be a tinker's cart drawn by a jennet, as the Irish call the offspring of a she-ass and a pony stallion – the opposite of a mule. And sometimes there would be a gypsy caravan.

Tinkers always had small, low-sided open carts, and the tinkers lived largely in the open, with at best a canvas sheet doing duty for a tent wherever they lodged in some road-side ditch. Their chief occupation was making and mending tinware.

The gypsy caravans were the well-known highly decorated roofed vehicles in which the gypsies lived and slept. If a gypsy caravan went past, I would hide in the bushes, because I was told to avoid gypsies as they were prone to kidnapping.

But there were two main interests to be served from my wall perch; fair-days were one of them.

Almost opposite the back of our stable yard, and the other side of the road, was the Athlone Fair Ground, a large open space of several acres outside the town on which the fairs took place. How often, I no longer recall – once a month? Once a quarter? I disremember, as the Irish say.

Animals would begin arriving during the night, and I would awaken in the early morning to the shouts of the drovers, the whack of their sticks on the bullocks' backs, and the patter of the animals' feet on the road. Any spare time I had between, before or after lessons, I flew to my ringside seat on the wall by the entrance gate to watch all that was going on. As the numbers built up on the Fair Ground, so did the noise: cattle bellowing, sheep bleating, pigs squealing, men shouting; and so did the smell, if the wind was from that direction – not an unpleasant or unhealthy smell, just the odours of the farmyard at full strength.

And sometimes we could persuade the grown-ups to take us to the fair itself. There we would see the bargaining: men in soiled raincoats gathered at the waist with a piece of string, 'ash plants' in their hands, tin-lidded clay pipes in their mouths, shouting at each other and gesticulating; and then a spit on the hand, and one man's hand slapped hard against the other man's upheld open palm, and the bargain was thus sealed.

From mid-morning on, the scene would go into reverse; droves of cattle and flocks of sheep, sold and coming away from the fair; gigs and traps and ass-carts with a newly bought young pig or young calf or a bunch of fowl in the back and a none too steady hand on the reins. By evening, except for the few last tipsy stragglers weaving their homeward way, all was quiet, and all that was left to us of the fair was the strong pervasive smell of cattle dung, and a road liberally decorated with splodges of animal droppings.

Those were lively occasions. They epitomised the hustle and bustle of the world, and the endeavours of men and women struggling with nature and with each other to earn a living and find some worthwhile meaning to life; as a child, I found them mighty stimulating, exciting and interesting. But the other, much more absorbing, much more deeply impressive and indeed disturbing, interest which I derived from my wall perch was not to do with life, but with death - funerals.

For me they had a compelling but horrifying fascination, and they affected me profoundly. As a funeral passed along that same road by our gate, life seemed suspended; the world was hushed; my soul stood still; there seemed but the barest thread, no more, between life itself and the inevitable grave.

A mile beyond our house, up our road, was the principal Athlone cemetery, Cornamagh, and the funeral processions coming out of the town passed our gate. Perhaps on the servants' grapevine, or because of some preparatory activity which I recognised, I would know when a funeral was due and would assume my perch on the wall by the gate. Then I would see the procession emerging from the town. A concentrated stillness would grip me. The rest of the world was blotted out. My mind and my eyes had room for one thing only, that slowly approaching, dark and sombre, doom-laden column of people. And soon it is coming round the bend where the road straightens out to go past our gate, and it wends its slow and dismal way straight towards me.

The large black hearse is in the lead, black as pitch, every inch of its ornately carved and decorated wood-work painted jet black. The black horses have black harness, and tall black plumes on their heads. They are walking slowly. On the driver's box, with his black reins, sits the black-clothed coachman, his tall top hat swathed in black crepe, the end of which hangs half a yard down over his shoulder. How, I wonder, could anyone undertake that gruesome task?

Now the hearse is passing me. If I have a cap on, I take it off, and hold it reverently against my heart until the hearse and the principal mourners have passed. I am a Protestant boy. We Irish Protestants do not cross ourselves: only Catholics do that. But I had learnt to do it privately, furtively, secretly and fervently, all by myself on my perch on the wall. No good, I thought, taking any chances with death. Above everything else in the world, I wanted to stay alive, and stay out of that hearse. Death seemed always at hand; there were in those days so many killer maladies which are now scarcely known – tuberculosis, diphtheria, scarlet fever to name but a few.

Now I can see the coffin through the glass side panels of the hearse. It is covered with wreaths. There are more on the roof. Morbid thoughts. Is it a man or a woman? Old or young? A child's coffin was smaller. A boy or girl? Pity, fear, a hundred eerie awesome thoughts jostle in my mind.

And now the hearse has passed, and here are the chief mourners all in black, in their black closed carriages, drawn by more black horses, and the weeping women in black veils with handkerchiefs to their eyes. Who, even at my tender age, could do other, in sheer reverence and decency, but sit totally still on my perch and share their grief with heartfelt compassion?

Any traffic – and there was little enough – that might be going in the opposite direction, pulled into the side of the road, stopped and, like me, crossed itself and held its headgear over its heart, at least until the hearse and principal mourners had gone by.

The carriages are gone, and now it is the people on foot, mournfully dark – clothed, perhaps four abreast, silent save for the swish and plod of their shuffling feet – quarter of a mile of them, half a mile, perhaps a mile long procession for a major funeral. And when all has gone, and emptiness has once more descended on our usually deserted road, I will come down from my wall perch, but the sense of melancholy and unease will linger with me.

There was an altogether different kind of funeral, more colourful –

no black, save for armbands – but no less mournful.

On the far bank, the west bank, of the Shannon river, on the farthest periphery of Athlone town, was a high-walled stronghold that held the British military garrison – Ireland being then a part of the United Kingdom. The units stationed there were infantry and artillery. There was also a military hospital. The Roman Catholic church now built within those walls did not then exist. Soldiers who died there were buried, with full British military honours, in the same Cornamagh cemetery, and the funeral processions took the same road past our gates. After the 1914/18 war started in August 1914, many wounded soldiers came to the Athlone Military Hospital, and some did not survive their wounds.

There was no need for prior news of a military funeral. I could hear it coming. Military funerals were accompanied by a band, and a long way off I could hear the slow, measured thud of the big drum, each explosive stroke, as the drummer struck it, sounding like the knell of doom. I would fly to the wall, drawn by the same horrific fascination that compelled me to watch the civilian funerals, and with mounting feelings of apprehensive interest and involvement as the cortege drew ever nearer. I hated death, but it would have been worse to let them go by, heard and unseen. I had a compulsive urge to be there to savour the horror at first hand.

No hearse this time, no silent shuffling crowd. A gun carriage drawn by three pairs of horses, a khaki-uniformed gunner driver riding one of each pair. The coffin on the gun carriage was draped with the Union Jack and the dead warrior's cap was on the lid. The few family mourners would come next, and then the slowly marching column of military comrades, arms reversed – about company strength, a hundred men or so; no shuffling feet here, but the crunch of the even tread of marching soldiers.

If it was the funeral of a mounted officer, his led charger would be there, his field boots reversed in the stirrups, and the saddle eloquently empty.

The band was always playing as they came out of the town, and passed by our gates. I thus came to know all the great funeral marches. They haunt me to this day, with Chopin's the most haunting of all. I can never hear it without graveyard shivers down my spine, and chilling recollections of the horrendous fascination of my silent and solitary vigil perched on that old wall.

And one thing was almost more distressing than all the rest. After the burial, the soldiers would come back down the road in quick time, the band playing cheerful tunes. Even to my childish mind, that was a desecration. How could they do it when their dead comrade was hardly cold in his grave? It seemed a gross and most offensive indecency. It was not universal. The Green Jackets never did it. Their respect for their dead was more enduring.

There was in those times a conventional parade of grief. Mourning. Blinds were pulled down in houses in which there had been a death, and black crepe was tied to door-knockers. Widows wore black or dark grey for the rest of their lives. Other female relatives wore black or dark clothes for so many months or weeks; and men, likewise, wore black ties for just as long, and in some cases black armbands. On the death of a royal personage, service officers wore black armbands in uniform for the prescribed period of court mourning. After a death in the family, family members would for weeks or months write their letters on black-edged letter paper and post them in black-edged envelopes. And if we had dirty finger nails we were asked scathingly if we were 'in mourning for the cat'.

Chapter 7

Outdoors - the Wide World

If you went out of our gate and turned left, you soon came to the level crossing of the Midland Railway. There was a narrow footpath along our side of the road, so there was no need to walk in the mud; that came later.

If you turned right out of the gate - the opposite direction - there was also a footpath. You soon passed under the bridge of the Southern Railway, and were heading for the town. But we will not go there yet. Let us turn left instead, and make towards the open country. That was the way we went for our daily walks. They were awful.

Sometimes, instead of crossing the railway at the level crossing, we would walk along the line for a bit towards Dublin, eighty miles away. I loved that. I would see how long I could balance on the rail and how fast I could go on it. I would jump from sleeper to sleeper, avoiding the ballast in between. It was quite safe. You could hear steam trains a long way off. Once I was allowed to put a penny on the line for a train to run over it. That flattened penny was a prized possession for a long time.

If, instead of an excursion up the line, we continued across the level crossing, there was one more house on our side of the road, Newcourt, where lived a retired army officer, Colonel Potts, and his wife. I visited them from time to time. He interested me greatly because he had spent many years in India. I now do not know whether it was he or someone else who gave me a splendid illustrated book on life in India. There were rajahs and maharajas; elephants and crocodiles; sahibs and memsahibs; soldiers in wonderful uniforms;

temples and mosques, native post-runners, mighty rivers and fabulously high and mysterious mountains, and many other wonders. For me it became a large part of a child's romantic vision of what life might eventually hold in store, though there were no plans for me at that time that might lead me to India.

In such a British garrison town as Athlone it would have been impossible to escape the influence of India. Those were the great days of the Empire, of which India was the greatest part, and there were many in the garrison, and in the vicinity of Athlone, who had served there.

But our walk took us on past Colonel Potts' domain.

Soon we were in open country where we had a choice of walks. If we took a particular turning to the left, we could do 'the one mile round': unutterably boring. If we took yet another turn to the left, we could do 'the two mile round': twice as long, twice as boring.

The discomfort of our clothes made it worse. Children wore boots, not shoes. They were always so tight that they had to be coaxed on with a shoehorn, a usually hurtful proceeding. The boots had little metal hooks round which the laces were threaded and then pulled too tight – hideously uncomfortable. Above the boots we wore tight-fitting, buttoned leather gaiters. The leather was soft, but to get the gaiters on each button had to be pulled into its opposite button-hole with a metal button-hook. As each button was levered into place with the hateful button-hook, it hurt more than the last one. Zips had not been invented. The daily donning of this foot and leg-wear was accompanied by our groans and squeals. We had not yet learnt to swear. The dressing was an ordeal for us, but it must have been a dreadful chore for the long-suffering grown-ups who had to endure our resistance to this daily martyrdom.

The purpose of all this armour plating was to protect us from the awful mud and wet of the rough roads for, once past the wall of Colonel Potts' property, the footpath petered out. Gum boots, or Wellington boots, had not then been invented. We wore only leather footwear, except for gym shoes at appropriate times – not for walks – which were canvas with rubber soles. Galoshes – rubber overshoes – had been invented, but we did not wear them until we were older.

There were variations on the one mile and two mile rounds, all, to us, equally boring. The country was an undulating sea of small fields, low banks and stone walls. A bull in a field would provide some interest, but I think the only thing that really lifted my heart was if a lonely ass, upon some self-chosen eminence, threw up his head, stretched out his neck, and started the awful gasping preludes to a loud and forlorn spasm of braying - nature's most exquisite example of bathos. It never failed to amuse me. It was one of the few sounds to disturb the quiet of the countryside. Tractors had not yet been invented. There were no aeroplanes. A motor car on a country road was a very rare sight. There was the singing of the songbirds, the cawing of rooks, the calls of men to their horses ploughing or pulling a cart; otherwise silence - nothing, of course, like combine harvesters.

There was one feature of that landscape that caught my imagination. Somewhere in it there was a particular 'green hill'. I identified it with the hymn lines:

> There is a green hill far away
> *Without* a city wall.

I used to wonder what my green hill would look like *with* a city wall. I pictured it in my mind surrounded by battlements, towers, arrow-slits and so on. Unfortunately green hills in our vicinity all lacked city walls, which made our walks seem even duller compared with lucky people in Bible lands, some of whose green hills evidently were provided with them.

The roads had to be kept in repair. Despite the virtual non-existence of motor traffic, whose speed is destructive of road surfaces, the iron-shod wheels of farm carts did break up the roads which were often badly pot-holed. There were two methods of repair, both using small stone chips the size of walnuts. What one might call running repairs were made by a man with a cart-load of stone chips and a shovel. Demarcation restrictions would probably require four men to do the job today. Then it was done by a well regulated partnership between the man and his horse.

When the cart got to the part of the road to be repaired, the man would stop the horse, take his shovel, go to the back of the cart and take off the tail board, being careful not to spill any of the stone chips onto the ground. Then, with the shovel, he would fill up each of the pot-holes within reach of the back of the cart. That done, he would shout to the horse, 'cum hup!' The horse would move slowly forward. When it had gone the required distance – about the length of itself and the cart, the road mender would shout 'woh-a!' and the horse would stop and patiently wait for the next 'cum-hup'. And so it went on all day, and it was left to the wheels of future traffic to roll in the little heaps of stone which had to be 'proud' in the pot-holes if they were to become level when rolled in. So, for days to come, the poor cottage ladies in their ass-carts would have an even more uncomfortable ride than usual on their hard plank seat as their unsprung carts bumped and swayed over the little heaps of stone.

If it was a case of major repairs, then our walk was really worth while, for that meant a steam-roller, its great fly-wheel spinning like fury, its brass-work gleaming, steam spouting from its pistons, the driver spinning the steering wheel like a top, and every now and then pulling a wire that caused a piercing note or two from the steam whistle above the cab; men shovelling stone in front of the machine and others watering it, and the great front roller crunching it into the road and leaving a beautiful level surface. That was worth watching, uncomfortable boots and tight gaiters momentarily forgotten.

Where did all those stone nuggets come from? There were machines known as 'stone crushers'. They may have had them on the main highways, but not on our minor roads. Our stone was prepared by hand. At intervals along the road were piles of big stones. Beside the pile sat a man on the heap of nuggets he had already prepared. He had a cap on his head the wrong way round, and wore goggles to protect his eyes. In his hand was a short, small-headed hammer. Holding a big stone in one hand and using the hammer very fast with the other he broke up the stone with astonishing dexterity into nuggets of the required size. They fell between his legs and, as he used up the big stones, he kept moving along on his bottom in the direction of the dwindling heap of big stones, leaving as he went a long neat bank of nuggets behind him. Down the years I have retained the impression that there was something penitential about that work. Maybe some of the men were released prisoners.

Those were our daily walks. Poor Miss Hatton. How did she endure it? But Saturday and Sunday were different.

That, however, was far from being the limit of our experience of the wide world. Motor cars had not become a normal part of family equipment. My father first got a driving licence in 1910, when he was thirty years old. Perhaps he got his first motor car that year but, as I have said, I do not remember a motor car stabled at Oldcourt. My mother did not learn to drive for nearly another twenty years, not I think until she bought her own first motor car. I doubt my father would have let her drive his.

My father's youngest sister, my Aunt Violet, got her first motor vehicle about the same time as my father.

And so it came about that, from an early age, we began to have the occasional experience of a drive in a motor car. They were very different then from now: very unreliable and the tyres punctured frequently with all the horse-shoe nails on the road; except for a very few large and expensive models, they were all open with a folding hood that could be put up if it rained; they had no windscreen wipers; and, of course, did not go very fast. Cruising on the roads of those days was hardly above twenty miles per hour. People used to list among their recreations in *Who's Who*, 'motoring'. The density of motor traffic was very low. Enterprising people of my father's generation, who could afford it, were taking to motoring. But it used to be said that a human being could not go above thirty miles per hour without blacking out.

We sometimes went to Correal, my father's former estate in Roscommon, some seven miles the far side, the west side, of Athlone. That was one of the places where I began to experience the Irish bogs, the Irish cottages and the lovely warm-hearted and welcoming people who lived in them. I was at that time too young to go shooting, but used to have little walks on the edges of the bogs. I have a particularly vivid recollection of one glorious bright frosty winter's morning when we went to Lough Whinchen, a low-lying boggy area with a small lake which was frozen over and, in trepidation, we walked out a long way on the hollow-sounding ice.

My father, having been brought up at Correal and many of the people there being his tenants, knew all the cottage folk, and we were made exceedingly welcome when we visited them. There was no ice to be broken there. They were universally glad to see him and were to me, as a child, warmly affectionate and interested in me. I enjoyed being in the cottages with their enormous open hearths with the sweet smell of burning turf (peat), and I might be given a delicious crust of freshly made bread generously buttered, or a new potato in a saucer with butter and salt. The right way to eat a potato in order to get the full delicious flavour is the way the Irish used to eat it – in the fingers with butter and salt, not cut with a knife or mixed with other food.

Other lovely excursions were to my grandmother's – my father's mother's – house, St Mark's. Two miles up the Shannon River, north of Athlone, is Lough Ree; a miniature inland sea, sixteen miles long and seven miles wide at its widest. Two or three miles up the lake on the right-hand side – the east side – was St Mark's. As I have already recorded, the house was set on a well timbered hill, in seventy acres of land, with endlessly beautiful and interesting views of the lake.

To visit my grandmother we either took the road round the east side of the lake through Glasson village, or we went by boat from Coosan Point some three miles north of where we lived. These expeditions might involve a motor car or a pony trap. Here we are in Oliver Goldsmith country. The Deserted Village, 'Sweet Auburn! loveliest village of the plain' is close to Glasson.

I found horse-drawn vehicles tedious. They were slow, and, if we went uphill, we had to get out and walk to lighten the burden of the horse or pony. They became lively only if we heard a motor car coming. Horses and ponies were not used to them. At best they would stand shivering with fright; in a worse situation they would shy and try to kick themselves out of the shafts and bolt. The antidote was to cover the horse's head with your coat and try to keep it calm while the terrifying source of all the noise went past.

Steam-rollers, likewise, gave rise to excesses of equine neuroses. With a coat over its head, sweating and shivering, the creature, prancing on its toes like a ballet dancer, would with difficulty be induced to sidle past the hissing and steaming monster, and it would then try to bolt as soon as it had got past.

There was one summer's day when my mother and I and Miss Hatton went by rowing-boat from Coosan Point to St Mark's - a couple of miles of rowing. Mollie and Sheelagh were taken by motor car. Out on the lake where we were, it was beautifully sunny. On the lake we always trolled a bait for perch and pike. That day we got into a shoal of perch off the south-east corner of the Hare Island and caught a lot of fish. But that was not our only excitement.

Inland to the east of us, where the motorists were making their way, the sky, by contrast with the sultry heat of our sunshine, had become black, as a large thunder-cloud built up. Before long there were brilliant flashes of lightning and the first mutterings of thunder soon gave way to great crashes which tore the sky above us and echoed round the clouds. A consultation: should we seek the shelter of the Hare Island, or row on the last half-mile to St Mark's? The latter was decided on, and we got there with no more than a few splashes of rain drops the size of pennies. The storm had veered off eastwards away from the lake.

But the motorists had been less lucky. They had been in the blackened middle of the storm. With the inadequate protection of the canvas motor car hood, they had been soaked by the tropical force of the driving deluges of rain; and, they said, the lightning had been all around them; balls of lightning had bounced down the road in front of the car. I have heard and read since on a number of occasions of this phenomenon of balls of lightning, but have never myself seen it.

St Mark's had its own pier and harbour and boat house, where boats were sheltered and safe from storms from any direction.

I loved St Mark's. The whole property, on the side of a tree-studded hill, looked westwards across the lake to the Roscommon shore, and all afternoon the sun glinted off the silver waters. If you approached by land you came by the narrow lane, winding its way up and down hill and round stone-walled corners from Glasson village two or three miles away. Iron gates whose special squeal, as you opened or closed them, still rings like music in my ears, led onto the quarter of a mile avenue running its entire length along the brow of the hill and in view of the lake.

At the time of which I am writing, before the 1914/18 War, the British garrison at Athlone based a large part of its social life on Lough Ree. There was a continuous coming and going of yachts, dinghies and rowing-boats; and all visitors by land or water were equally welcome at St Mark's. That sounds all very well, but my Aunt Violet told me years later that she felt a constant anxiety for the young and inexperienced officers who were naturally tempted to enjoy to the full the amenities of the lake. It was far from being a safe place. There were dangerous submerged shoals and rocks; and sudden storms could blow up, or strong gusts of wind that could capsize a boat. For instance, my Aunt Blossie's diary:

Saturday, 2 August 1917
Centreboard capsized in Lake. 2 Lieuts., Simpson and Livesay, were drowned. Lieut. Pettigrue drifted to the Hare Island clinging to the boat and was saved.
Sunday, 17 August
Lieut. Simmonds' body found on shore of Green Island Sandy Bay. [She had the name wrong the first time.]
Monday 18 August
Lieut. Livesay's body was washed up on Hare Island.

That was a funeral I would not have forgotten had I witnessed it – a double military funeral – but I was not there. Owing to circumstances connected with World War I, we were not at Oldcourt at that time.

My paternal grandfather had died before I was born, and before his wife, my grandmother, moved to St Mark's, but there she and four unmarried daughters, my Magan aunts, kept open house. My grandmother was a lovely, sweet-tempered, placid person, who was endlessly and warmly patient with us, and kind to us as children – her only grandchildren in a sense because her eldest son, Percy Magan, who was the only other member of the family to have children, had settled in America and she never saw his family.

My four Magan aunts were Blossie, Muriel, Rachel and Violet. I knew them all exceedingly well, and was very fond of them. I often stayed with them. It can indeed be said that they were part of the furniture of my life. Beyond calling them Aunt, and treating them with the natural courtesy due to aunts, our relationship with each other was close and relaxed, free, friendly and full of laughs and jokes. Only Rachel married.

They were all useful and interesting people. Blossie, the eldest, perhaps in emulation of Florence Nightingale, became a trained hospital nurse. She was tall with a good figure, and must have looked splendid in a nurse's uniform. She did not do it for a living. All the sisters had independent means. She did it as a contribution to people less fortunate than herself. She nursed throughout the years of World War One. Like all my Magan aunts, she had a warm nature, a sense of adventure and a splendid sense of humour.

Muriel, the next sister, I believe also had a nurse's training. She spent her life looking after an aged and otherwise lonely sea captain. When he died she came home and ran my grandmother's house for her. She was a born organiser, but was very discreet and not bossy. In any company she would have risen to a position of command. She was exceptionally attractive and we as children adored her. Sadly she died all too young while I was still a schoolboy.

Rachel was the most feminine of the four sisters, and the most appreciative of pretty things. She ran my grandmother's flower garden. Like her younger sister Violet and my father, she was a good yachtsman. She was a very active member of the Irish Agricultural Organisation Society (IAOC) which aimed to help small farmers to help themselves through the acquisition of new and better skills, up-to-date methods, better stock and seed, co-operative purchasing and marketing and protection against those who, like the 'Gombeen Men', preyed on them ruthlessly. Rachel, in a house provided by her father in Roscommon, established a Home Industry Society for local girls, teaching in particular lace making. Although she was the only one of the sisters who married, she had no children.

Violet, the youngest sister, though quiet and restrained, had the most compelling character and personality of the four sisters. She became well-known throughout central and western Ireland for her work on behalf of the AIOC in which she specialised in poultry. In addition she was the principal figure in the estate office which she and my father and two friends set up to run the former large Magan estates and the estates of other people who, for reason of old age or other problems, could not continue to run them themselves. That, as will be revealed later, was to become a hazardous occupation. She was extremely efficient at business, and in that field could hold her own with professional men. She was a magnet for children. She did not pay them too much attention, but they loved her and the droll things that she used to say. She was penetratingly observant of other people, and often very funny about them without being unkind. There was ancient country blood in her veins and all her adult life she kept horses, dogs and cattle. She was for years probably the most successful helmsman in the regattas on Lough Ree. She was also the Honorary Secretary to the committee of the South Westmeath Foxhounds – in effect she ran the hunt's administration. After my grandmother's death, she took over her beautiful home, St Mark's, and spent the remainder of her life there.

My grandmother had, to help her to care for the property, such a man of all works as was known to every household of that kind in Ireland. Irish countrymen are extraordinarily versatile. They all have a sound practical understanding of mixed farming. They can all do such gardening as is necessary. They all have more than a handyman's knowledge of the maintenance of buildings, walls and so on. Indeed many build their own houses, doing all the work themselves with their own hands. They have a deep understanding of livestock, horses, cattle and sheep; and, if they live near water, as many do in that wet country, they are competent in boats, and at such fishing as may be appropriate to their circumstances.

Such a man was my grandmother's man of all works, Pat Callaghan. At that time he had another man named Coombes, whom I do not remember and a 'young fellah', Mike Hopkins, even more versatile than himself, to help him. After St Mark's was burnt, as I shall relate, my Aunt Violet took the place over and eventually made a small cottage in the yard for herself. Mike Hopkins stayed with her to help her for the rest of his life, and she eventually left the St Mark's property to him. Sadly he died a few years ago aged ninety-one, but his widow and his family still live at St Mark's.

In my grandmother's time, Pat Callaghan himself had a cottage in the yard at St Mark's. The yard is the remains of an ancient monastic building. Some of its walls must be a thousand years old. There is, too, a lovely old walled garden where the wallflowers grow like weeds on the walls.

Pat Callaghan's cottage is another Irish cottage of which I have the most heart-warming recollections. Pat Callaghan's wife Ellen treated me as her son. My memories of Ellen give me a complete understanding of the fostering of children practised in the old Irish septs. It came naturally to warm-hearted Irish country-women, like her, to mother all children as though they were their own. Many years later when, as a young man, I was posted to join the Forces in India, and I went to say goodbye to Ellen, she saw no reason to suppress her feelings. She was sure she would never see me again and, with tears streaming down her cheeks, she called down blessings on me from the Blessed Virgin and all the saints. It worked, because we both lived to be reunited.

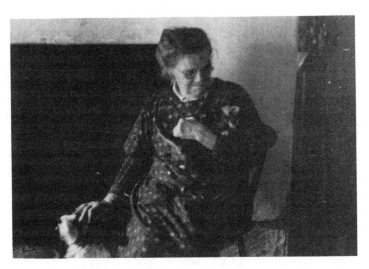

Ellen Callaghan, St Mark's Cottage, Glasson, Co. Westmeath

She was old-fashioned. She was not very tall – stocky one might say – and she always wore the universal dress of Irish country women at that time – a full black skirt ankle length, a black bodice and a black shawl over her shoulders or, when she went out, over her head if necessary.

Some places – some spots, I should say – hold a particular attraction all their own. Such were the stone steps leading down from the front door at St Mark's to the avenue. They were a place to congregate, a place to sit, perhaps on a rug, a place where I played as a small child under the watchful eye of my grandmother. They were irresistible on a warm afternoon in the sunshine, with their wide view across the ever-moving, silver-glinting lake. Years later I used to sit there with my Aunt Violet and put the world to rights, while the sun sank across the opposite Connaught shore into the light westward sky that reflected the distant Atlantic ocean.

My father and his sisters, having been brought up at Correal in Roscommon, the other side of the lake, and not far from it, had long been used to semi-aquatic lives. My father owned a yacht named *Violet* after his youngest sister and Violet, herself, had her own yacht. My Aunt Rachel had a bright scarlet 'centre-board' boat. The character of Athlone itself was largely determined by the wide Shannon River which flowed through the midst of it and was a boating highway. Thus, our early lives as children became in part dominated by water. Rowing regattas on the river, where it ran through the town, with men in white singlets, with their long oars and slim racing boats, and beautiful sailing regattas on the lake, with the water dotted with white sails, became a part of our early consciousness. To us, a world without regattas would have been unthinkable.

It was perhaps the first time that I ever went sailing that my father took us in his yacht one warm afternoon from Athlone up the Shannon to go for a sail on Lough Ree. We never got there. There was not enough wind to blow out a match. We tacked backwards and forwards across the river, making, I suppose, a yard or two each time. I was utterly bored but, worse than that, I was hideously embarrassed by the awful noises my father kept making. He kept bawling out things like 'Lee-oh!' and other nautical expletives that meant nothing to me. He could have been heard two miles away, in conditions in which a whisper would have done; and I myself was always being told not to shout. But I was to learn that reticence was something for which my father had little or no use. He *liked* to be heard two miles away.

There was a Sunday morning, perhaps in 1915, when my Aunt Violet and I went by boat a short way up the Shannon from Athlone to a boat-builder's yard where her yacht was up on the stocks having its hull below the waterline polished with graphite. There we chanced to meet a well-known Athlone solicitor, Mr Murtagh, on some mission no doubt connected with his own boat. He was always impeccably, and very fashionably, dressed. He had a strong voice and, in Irish intonations, spoke in an emphatic manner not uncommon with Irishmen.

On this occasion, it was with pronounced emphasis that he imparted his gruesome news to my aunt. He had, he said, just come from screwing down the lid on Mr Kelly's coffin. Mr Kelly was a much liked and respected bank manager who had died all too young. The funeral was to be the next day. I knew Mr Kelly and his wife well; they had been very kind to me. Thoughts of him in his coffin haunted me until I climbed onto my wall perch next day to watch the cortege. It was a particularly moving funeral and remains vividly in my mind because, behind the coffin, came limping on a stick and in uniform, and with a black armband, Mr Kelly's elder son, Eddy, just home wounded from the trenches in France.

Mention of Mr Murtagh the solicitor brings to mind a story of two of the other Athlone solicitors. A man considering litigation called on one of them and explained his problem. The solicitor said that it was not the sort of case he usually handled, but he could recommend his colleague Mr X, whose office was at the other end of the town. On the way there, the man had second thoughts, and felt he should sleep on the matter. By next morning he had concluded that he should not go ahead with his suit. However, the first solicitor had given him a letter of introduction to the second solicitor, so he decided to open it to see in what terms one solicitor introduced a potential customer to another. The letter was short and to the point:

Dear X,
Here's a plump pigeon; pluck him.
　　　Yours truly
　　　　Y

There was a litigious family who had their various residences in the vicinity of Athlone, and who were habitually carrying on law suits against each other. Let us call them the Loverings. On one occasion in the list of cases to be heard there appeared this one:

'Lovering versus Lovering for the trespass of a duck.'

Rathrobin in the King's County

We used sometimes to visit other people's houses. I do not remember that we ever had a children's party of our own, but perhaps we did. Although I have rather hazy recollections of children's parties in other houses, one in particular still haunts me.

My mother had a nice set of silver buttons. She conceived the idea that they would look good on a brown velvet suit for me. So the suit was duly made, I think by herself. I suppose she had Little Lord Fauntleroy in mind. I hated him and the suit, in which I felt ridiculous. They thought I looked sweet. I did not want to look sweet. Boys may like to look fierce, but not sweet. Dress them as Long John Silver, and they will be delighted. At all events I was made to go to a party in this, to me awful, suit, and I spent all the time I could hiding behind a curtain. But now I think how horrid it was of me to disappoint my lovely mother who had gone to all that trouble, as she must have thought, to do something nice for me.

Occasionally we went much further afield. Sometimes we went to visit my great-uncle Middleton Biddulph, and his English wife, Aunt Vera, at their home, Rathrobin, in the King's County.

Like so many of the Irish Ascendency, Middleton had as a young man been commissioned into the British Army, the 5th Northumberland Fusiliers (The Fighting 5th), with whom he served the whole of his career until his retirement with the rank of Lieutenant-Colonel.

In 1891 he married Vera Flower, fourteen years younger than himself. They had no children. She was the sister of a brother officer, and was a member of the Stratford-on-Avon Flower brewing family. Her father was Sir William Flower, a distinguished doctor who had fought in the Crimean War and who eventually became director of the National History Museum and President of the Royal Zoological Society.

Both Middleton and Vera were very starched upper-class Victorians, very unlike my easy-going Magan aunts. Middleton was indeed a typical dutiful late Victorian gentleman. He was, in his retirement, a Justice of the Peace, Deputy Lieutenant and High Sheriff of the King's County. While maintaining the highest conventional old-fashioned standards of his class, he was also very alive to, and interested in, modern inventions and developments. To give some instances, he installed the most modern plumbing in Rathrobin; he was an early user of a mechanical tractor on his home farm; and he was a keen and good photographer who has left us many interesting photographs of the period.

He was also a scholarly man. He kept up the classics, and had a splendid library of several thousand books, and he kept abreast of modern thinking, Darwin, Ruskin, Newman and others. He was a conventional member of the Church of Ireland, a church warden who believed in Sunday observances.

Aunt Vera was unbending upper-class Victorian English. She never succumbed to less rigid Irish ways. Rathrobin was as English a home as she could make it. Her father's home in London had been a parade of the great Victorians. Darwin, Lister, Huxley, Longfellow, Tennyson, Browning, Dean Farrar and Charles Kingsley were among his colleagues and friends. One of Vera's three uncles was Astronomer Royal for Scotland; the other two were both knighted for their services. One of her cousins was Baden-Powell, founder of the Scout Movement. Those were the influences that moulded her, a far cry from fox hunting and snipe shooting in rural Ireland. Although rigidly conventional, she had a sweet and gentle nature. Perhaps in her own secret understanding she was homesick in those very different Irish surroundings; perhaps in her heart of hearts, 'sick for home, she stood and wept among the alien corn'.

Uncle Middleton and Aunt Vera were kind to me, and he used to give me half-crowns which was generous, but he also used to scare me by asking me sudden and unexpected questions. 'Say your seven times table.' I knew my seven times table perfectly well, but to be asked to say it by Uncle Middleton out of the blue put a severe strain on my young nerves. I had to be at all times very strictly on my best behaviour at Rathrobin, and it was a relief eventually to be able to depart through the front gates and breath freely again.

We used also to go to Killyon Manor in the County Meath. It had been part of the former large Magan estates which, under a badly drawn will, had passed into other hands. But my father and his sister Violet looked after the estates for the new owners, who were English,

Killyon Manor

and we had the run of all the properties. The big house at Killyon was not lived in at that time, but was looked after by John Curley, the game-keeper, and his wife and family, who lived in the back yard.

When we went to Killyon, we stayed in the fully furnished pebble-dashed house opposite the front gate. It was later sold, and we then began to use the big house as a holiday home.

We loved Killyon with its river and woods, and were great friends with all the people who worked there. Polly Shanley, the wife of Tom Shanley, the steward, was a particular favourite. She was a very motherly woman, and we simply loved her. She used to come and help in our house, and sometimes she would ask us to tea in her house in the Killyon stable yard. My deep affection for her was bolstered by hardly less respect because I concluded from my observations that she must be very rich. I had heard that rich people had 'pots of money', and I noticed that she kept her loose change in a pot on her kitchen dresser.

When I was five or six years old, a tragedy happened at Killyon. John Curley, the keeper, and his wife had a large family, I think six or seven children. Diphtheria struck the family, and in a few days, John's wife and all the children except one, a boy named Con, died. Later John married again, but he had no more children. His second wife Anne used to cook for us when we were holidaying in Killyon Manor.

We never left Ireland. Few people thought of taking short holidays abroad in those days. But I do recall one holiday on Achill Island in the west of Ireland. We stayed at the hotel in Dugort, run by a Mr and Mrs Sheridan. I viewed him with particular respect because I was told that his family was related to Lord Nelson. There was a grown-up son, a splendid person and great seaman, Brinsley. I think he was killed in the first war. And there were two daughters – Hope, who ran the hotel for many years afterwards, and Kiddo, an adolescent tomboy at that time. While we were staying there, she got into trouble. In some prank, she threw a large black iron cooking pot – such as was common in Ireland – off the end of the pier and into quite deep water. What's more, I think it belonged to the police – thus heaped upon transgression was insult to the majesty of the law.

The matter was considered with due solemnity and hoary head-shakings, and it was finally decreed that, as Kiddo had deposited the pot on the floor of the ocean, where it was plainly visible, through the gin-clear water, being gently caressed by fronds of seaweed, she must contrive to recover it.

So early on a calm sunny morning, after breakfast, we all trooped down to the pier to see the crime expiated. The culprit, not exactly in chains, but in a blue bathing costume and wrapped in a white towel, and in the bare feet which she customarily wore, was escorted – looking quite insufficiently contrite – to the scene of the crime.

In a moment she threw off the towel, and her slim figure plunged in off the pier and broke the tranquil lapping surface of the ocean. She had spent as much of her short life in the Atlantic as out of it, and no sooner was she in the water than she became a seal. Down went her head, up went her legs, and she swam effortlessly to the bottom, grabbed the handle of the pot and re-surfaced with it. It was an unforgettably beautiful display of lissom youth performing perfectly in an element in which she was as much at home as she was on dry land. I did not, of course, think of it in those terms at that time of my own young life, but the scene remains vividly imprinted on my mind, and I can describe it thus today.

Puddles, heaps of mud, piles of stones are magnets to small children. A little road ran past the front of the Dugort Hotel, and ran on the short distance down to the pier. There was, of course, no traffic except the occasional ass-cart, or panniered beautiful little Connemara ponies carrying turf. The far side of the road from the hotel was some kind of little garden, where a few brave and hardy plants struggled against the Atlantic gales and salt spray from the breakers, for a stunted existence.

One morning I crossed the road. There on the garden path was a lovely heap of something to get into and kick about. I was wearing sandals. So, in I jumped and gave the stuff a good kick. I came out even quicker, and perhaps screaming. Someone early that morning had 'taken a notion' – as they say in Ireland – to clean out the large turf fires from the hearths, and had deposited the powdery ashes in a heap on the garden path, perhaps with a view to putting them on the flower beds as a fertiliser when they had cooled down. To me they looked white and fluffy and irresistibly attractive to play with, but underneath they were red hot. My feet were badly burnt, and I padded about in bandages for several days.

There were lovely beaches on Achill Island, and exciting cliffs and rock pools; and, most memorable of all, the charming cowrie shells of which we collected masses.

Although I was no more than five or six years old at that time, that holiday in Achill implanted in me the seeds of a great love of the West of Ireland. I know no other place in the world that is more hauntingly beautiful – and I have seen a lot of the world.

Chapter 8

Saturdays

There were two days in the week that were different from the remainder, Saturday and Sunday.

On Saturday morning there were no lessons. We received our pocket-money - one penny each. The penny of those days was one two hundred-and-fortieth of a pound. In other words it took 2.4 of those pennies to make one of our modern pennies. But intrinsically money was worth more, and our old penny would buy twenty times as much as today.

Armed with our pennies, we would walk with Miss Hatton into the town of Athlone where we usually went to a little grocer's shop run by a Mr and Mrs Boyd, Protestants from the north of Ireland, very nice people, who always treated us very kindly. Their shop was a little above St Mary's Protestant church, on the corner at the top of the main street where it widens into a sort of square.

There we would buy sweets - acid drops were the favourite, perhaps because we got more for our money, and Mr and Mrs Boyd would add a few extra. Or we would buy 'surprise packets', diamond shaped packs of not very nice sweets with, in each pack, a 'surprise', such as a diminutive spinning top.

If it was a fair day, the square would be full of carts and cattle and other animals, of shouting and, by mid-day, tipsy men, and an immense, but not disagreeable to country people, smell of dung.

We usually did some other shopping in Athlone for the house. At the Boyds' it might be a pound or two of sugar. Sugar was brown, white, lump or loaf. Loaf sugar was a large cone weighing several pounds suspended by a string down the middle, round which the grains had crystallised. It would be taken down from where it was hanging, and the requisite amount broken off with a hammer. Virtually nothing was pre-wrapped, and it was long before the days of plastic or cellophane. Paper bags, too, were not generally used in grocer's shops. There were square pieces of paper – deep blue or brown. People working at the counter wound them dextrously into a cone, poured in the sugar or rice or whatever it might be, weighed it and added or subtracted a little, and then neatly folded in the top. In effect, it made a perfectly secure paper bag.

I suppose Miss Hatton liked to have an opportunity to visit the shops, so we would spend almost all Saturday morning in the town, and we got to know a lot of the shop people. That, no doubt, also gave Miss Hatton a chance for a little more company than she could have in our home. There were excellent shops including Flemmings,

The Ascendancy goes for a picnic

The Ascendancy goes for a picnic

the chemists, where the whole Flemming family worked – more Northern Protestants. At Burgess's, the drapers, they had overhead runners where the little boxes carrying money and change whizzed to and fro along wires between the counters and the central cashier's desk. There we used to buy bootlaces and other small things – buttons, reels of cotton – and I used to be intrigued to watch elderly country people trying out spectacles. There was a basket of steel rimmed spectacles on the counter which people used to buy for, I suppose, about sixpence. Perhaps they were no more than magnifying glasses, but it was the nearest most of the country people ever got to an optician.

Foy's had toys, bicycles and sports gear. Nearby was Milligan's the tailor's where my father got his excellent hard-wearing, country clothes. Tailors were a part of every community, and much clothing was hand-made. Indeed, it used to be contemptuously said of a piece of clothing that was not tailor-made, that it 'was bought off the peg'. Clothes were also much thicker than they now are because, as there was no heating in vehicles and little or no background heating in houses, there was more need to wear warmer clothing than now. Anoraks had not been invented. Instead we wore heavy tweeds. A singularly revolting garment of winter wear, worn next to the skin, and tickly and scratchy, was 'combinations' – known as 'combs', a woollen garment combining both vest and pants. To put on a garment inadvertently inside out was said to bring good luck.

Cobblers were also a part of every community, and much footwear was also hand-made. The cobbler would make a last in the shape of a person's foot on which he could build footwear of the right size. He also did all boot and shoe repairs. Boots were more commonly worn than shoes.

From Boland's, the bakers at the top of the town, there was always a delicious smell of newly baked bread, and they had a smart, well-turned out, horse-drawn van. At the other end of the town was Lipton's where we used sometimes to buy bacon, and had the pleasure of watching it cut, with a metallic clang, by a spinning circular knife. It tasted much nicer than our own home-cured, over-salted, bacon, so my mother saw to it that we only got it occasionally as a special treat.

At Lipton's we were near the river, and we would walk down to the quay and look at the boats and the boat builder's yards and people fishing, and it was an endless pleasure to watch the water pouring over the beautiful weir that spans the Shannon there.

Sometimes we would go to 'the office' in Northgate Street. At the time that my father sold his Roscommon estate, and he and his sister Violet took over the running of the former Magan estates – some 20,000 acres – they set up for themselves an estate office. This they did in partnership with two friends, George Moony of the Doon and Arthur Handcock, Lord Castlemaine's younger son. My father also took out an auctioneer's licence. By degrees, other people came to value their knowledge and experience, and they thus found themselves with a number of estates on their hands. My father and my Aunt Violet were also, as I have said, very active in the co-operative movement to help mainly small peasant proprietors and tenants, which had been set up, and was directed by, the Hon. Sir Horace Plunket, whose principal collaborator was Father Tom Findlay. The work that my father and my aunt did for it was mostly carried on from their Northgate Street estate office in Athlone.

On our Saturday morning rounds, we would call at the office to see my Aunt Violet. We would make a nuisance of ourselves, no doubt, for a few minutes, having a go on her typewriter, and would then be hustled out, pounding down the dimly-lit wooden stairway. But my Aunt Violet was always very patient and tolerant, and we loved her dearly.

Nearly two decades later when Ireland was in a turmoil of IRA activity, she was still running the estate agency on her own, and was looking after a number of estates for friends and relations, one of them being the Rathrobin estate of my great-uncle Middleton Biddulph. In order to put an end to such loyalist estates, the IRA were burning big houses; and landlords, and particularly their agents, were under threat.

The roads were often made impassable by the IRA with holes blown in bridges and felled trees across the road. Aunt Violet used therefore to do her longer journeys to visit estates by train, taking her bicycle with her. One day, after a visit to Rathrobin, she was cycling the seven miles back to Tullamore to catch the train when she was attacked by the IRA and pulled from her cycle. Poison was poured down her throat; she was tied up and thrown into a wood and left for dead. She was, however, still alive, and struggled free and regained the road where she was found semi-conscious and taken to a doctor in Tullamore. She was very ill for many months and never fully recovered her health, but she defied the IRA and went back to the estate office, managing it until she was seventy years of age.

Northgate Street had other attractions. Our doctor, the avuncular Dr Dobbs, friend and much loved and respected benefactor of everyone, rich and poor alike, lived there. Mr Symonds, the photographer who from time to time took our photos, had his shop and studio there. Calls on him were frequent to enable Miss Hatton to consult him about photographic problems.

In Northgate Street also was the Longworth Hall. I once went to a concert there to hear my mother sing. I suppose it was some charity show. She used to accompany Percy French in charity concerts. He is, of course, well known as an extraordinarily versatile and gifted artist, writer and, in his day, entertainer, author of 'The Mountains of Mourne' and many other well-known Irish songs. After charity concerts the stage would be littered with his lightning sketches, and my mother always regretted not having gathered some of them up, but she bequeathed me a charming little sunset bog scene water-colour of his which I suppose he gave her. His first song, whistled and sung from one end of the earth to the other, written when he was an undergraduate at Trinity College, Dublin, was 'Abdallah Bulbul Ameer'. He failed to copyright it, and it was pirated by a London firm of music publishers who published a slightly altered version and scooped the pool.

Another feature of Northgate Street was the Athlone Woollen Mill. From behind its great gates would come strange noises and clankings. John MacCormack, the famous Irish tenor, once worked there. At times, perhaps if we were there at noon when they may have been shutting down for the weekend, we would see all the mill girls come pouring out. They wore black dresses, and had black woollen shawls over their heads, and bare feet, and they hurried home up the main street towards Irishtown. That was not their mill uniform. It was their everyday dress.

We sometimes went to Irishtown. It was a poor low-lying area of the town near the river, and I dimly recollect that the houses could get flooded if the river rose very high in a big flood. The people were poor there, and the mill girls worked hard.

Underlining the poverty and some of the depravity that then went with it, were familiar sights that, in the improved social conditions of today, have largely disappeared. Drunk men were frequently seen lurching down the streets, and we were pulled out of their way. Pitiful bare-footed children, shivering in their inadequate rags, were a common sight. There was much spitting in public – a highly dangerous habit when tuberculosis was rampant, as it then was, and there was no cure for it. As late as the 1930s there were notices in all London buses: 'Spitting prohibited. Penalty £5.' Today no-one spits.

Spitting reminds me that in those days some working class men not only smoked tobacco but also chewed it. The chewing tobacco was called 'twist'. It was sold in rope form about the thickness of a finger. Men bit the end off the piece of rope and chewed it and then spat it out, so the pavements were strewn with the expectorated chewed twist.

Another sight no longer to be seen is wooden legs. There were then no artificial limbs. A lost leg was replaced with a short pole-like piece of wood – commonly called a peg-leg – which fitted into a holder that was strapped to the stump of the leg. There were no replacements for amputated arms. Men wore the empty sleeve sewn into their pocket. If the amputation was low down, the hand might be replaced with a hook.

Continuing our Saturday morning tour of the attractive and interesting market town of Athlone, we would sometimes go across the wide river bridge over the Shannon. At times salmon could be seen lying in the water below. The far end of the bridge was dominated by ancient fortifications, and the great gateway and high walls of the British military barracks.

On the far side of the bridge, under the walls of the old fort, was the fish market where the Islandmen brought their fish from the lake. The most common were perch, baskets of them, and barrels of live wriggling eels, a favourite Irish delicacy - delicious stewed in milk. There would be bream and pike, and a few trout as well. The eels were caught on long night lines, and in eel nets at the weir at Athlone. The other fish were caught mainly in draw nets. The Islandmen were a community who lived on the islands in Lough Ree and kept very much to themselves. They had no doubt lived there for many centuries.

There was a day when we arrived at Coosan Point to go by boat to St Mark's at the moment that the men were 'drawing' Lord Castlemaine's draw in the lake there. We watched it come in, and there was great excitement because it contained, among the other thrashing fish in the end of the net as it came ashore, an exceptionally large trout.

Another large fish that remains in my mind was caught at the Hodsons' home, Twyford, which was not far from Athlone. My mother took me there one day, and as we approached the house we met a man with an enormous pike slung over his back. My mother asked him where he had got it. He said he hadn't: he was carrying it home for 'Miss Nellie' - one of the Hodson sisters - who had just caught it.

The remainder of the town beyond the bridge - the Connaught side of the town - we hardly knew. It seemed a different place. But there was one shop there that was familiar to us, Lyster's, the flourishing hardware shop. The Lysters were a great sporting family. They took a prominent part in the yacht racing on Lough Ree, and were strong supporters of the local hunt - the South Westmeath Hounds, whose kennels were just outside Athlone.

Sometimes we would be in the town in the evening. It would then be full of British soldiers in uniform strolling about, shopping I suppose, and picking up girls. The Gunners always looked particularly smart in their tight tunics, their riding breeches with the buckskin strappings on the inside of the knees pipe-clayed white, and always carrying their long riding whips.

There were two cinemas in the town, and there we saw very early films, Charlie Chaplin and others. There were no colour films, and no soundtracks, no talking; they were silent but there might be some accompaniment on a piano. I also recall what I think must have been an amateur performance of Gilbert and Sullivan's *HMS Pinafore.*

Circuses used to come to the town, a long procession of painted and decorated horse-drawn caravans, very like the horse-drawn caravans in which gypsies lived. The big round tent – the big top – would be erected on the Fair Ground, quite close to our house. Inside were circular tiers of wooden benches, leaving gaps for entrances and exits, and with a special gap for the performers and animals. In the centre was a sawdust ring for the performers. Hanging from the roof was an assortment of horizontal bars, rings and so on.

I only half enjoyed circuses. They did not excite me. I would not have minded being told that I would never see another. I loved the jugglers, and the acrobats at their most acrobatic, but I did not enjoy the seemingly dangerous acts. Clowns I never liked. I thought them grotesque. It would be impossible to be as close as we were in the circus 'big-top' to lions and tigers without a sense of wonder and awe and apprehension. And we could not fail to admire the courage and skill of the men and girls who went into the cages with those snarling brutes and forced them to submit to their will. But it was hardly enjoyment. It was too close to pitiless and merciless nature in the raw. The quick-moving equestrian acts and trick ridings I loved, and the pistol shot cracks of the smart ring-master's whip.

We used to arrive home at Oldcourt from our Saturday morning visits to the town just in time for lunch. We would go straight upstairs and take off our overcoats and boots and get into house shoes. That detail I mention because what happened on one particular morning fixes it in my mind.

Not far from St Mark's and a little further up the lake was Portlick Castle, and there lived Mr and Mrs Robert Smythe (pronounced Smith) and their daughter Harriet (Harrie).

One Saturday morning we had just arrived back from the town, and were halfway up the stairs, still in our outdoor clothes, when Mr Smythe, who had ridden in from Portlick on his bicycle, appeared at our open hall door in his cycling clothes – knickerbockers, stockings, boots, Norfolk jacket and cloth cap.

He had a strong Irish accent, and he shouted after us as we went up the stairs, 'St Mark's is bur'rned. St Mark's is bur'rned.'

St Mark's was indeed burnt. To quote from the diary entry of Saturday, 9 August 1913, of my aunt Emily Magan, my father's eldest sister 'Blossie':

At about 10 minutes to 9 a.m., just as I came out of my bath, the parlourmaid discovered the roof was on fire. Callaghan went up and broke some slates, found the rafters blazing furiously from end to end, and his cap was burned off his head. Having neither help nor appliances it was impossible to put it out. So, mother went out in her dressing gown, and the rest of us - that is Rachel, Violet, self, Coombes, Callaghan, Lizzie and Bridget, proceeded to save what we could. The dining room roof fell in at 9.10, and the roof of mother's room a few minutes later. She lost everything except her watch, spectacles, brushes and a few underclothes. The flames hunted us from room to room, and when all the roof was down we went into the basement till the floors above us fell in. In an hour and a half the house was a blackened ruin.

Then Miss Daniels [the nearest neighbour] and her men appeared, Johnnie Quigley, Willy Duffy (from the Hare Island) and others helped us, but were practically too late to be of much use. Robert Smythe . . . appeared . . . and then rode on his bicycle to Athlone . . .

A telegram was sent to my father by Bob Smythe as he cycled through Glasson village. My father happened to be away from home but managed to get to St Mark's before long. As soon as the news got around, other friends turned up to help. My grandmother came to stay with us. My aunts and the servants were put up by various neighbours.

Despite the speed with which the fire spread, a remarkable amount was saved out of the house though, of course, a lot also was lost. My grandmother and my aunts and the staff seem to have been exceedingly brave in the way they remained in the house trying to save things while the burning roof and floors were falling in all around them.

Although the lake was only a hundred yards away, it was also a hundred feet below the house, and there was no way of getting sufficient water up to deal with the fire. Perhaps the nearest fire engine was in Athlone, nine miles away, and anyway there was no telephone to summon help. House telephones were unknown in country places in those days. The fire engine was also probably horse-drawn.

After the fire, my grandmother and my aunts lived for a year or so at our old family home, Killyon Manor, Co. Meath, until they found another house to suit them near Athlone, which was where they wanted to be.

Among the things that were lost was a little grey-green Chinese jade figure belonging to my grandmother. At some later time it was found among the ashes, quite unscathed. My grandmother gave it to me. She told me that it was the third fire that it had survived. It is still numbered among my small possessions, reminding me of her, of St Mark's, of that Saturday morning halfway up the stairs at Oldcourt, and of Bob Smythe, his strong Irish accent, and his bicycle.

My father always mounted his bicycle by putting his left foot on the left pedal, and throwing his right leg over the saddle once the machine was under way. But Mr Smythe and Arthur Handcock did it differently.

In those days men's cycles had a piece of metal, three or four inches long, sticking out of the left hand side of the hub of the rear wheel. It was called 'the step'. You could put your left foot on that, shove off with your right foot, and then mount the cycle from the rear. That was how Mr Smythe and Arthur Handcock did it. It looked very awkward and unsafe, and I never learnt to do it.

There were still a few bicycles around with 'fixed wheels' - no freewheel. That is to say that, so long as the bicycle was moving, the pedals kept going round. They were very awkward to ride.

I do not know whether children's bicycles had then been made. We did not have any. But I learnt to ride at an early age on grown up men's cycles just by putting my right leg under the bar and doing without a seat.

So far as I recall, Saturdays, from lunchtime on, were the same as other days except that, the grown-ups being free for the weekend, there might be some outing in which we would be included.

Chapter 9

Sundays

Sunday was the most boring day in the week. It is perhaps not true to say that it was deliberately made boring, in order to be good for our souls. Maybe it was the other way round. What was judged to be good for our souls just was boring.

We had to wear Sunday clothes. They were tighter and more uncomfortable than week-day ones. I do not remember all the restrictions, but there were things we were not allowed to do, things with which we were not allowed to play. To touch a pack of cards on a Sunday was sinful in the extreme.

It was my mother who imposed the Sunday regime. I think my father thought it a lot of tommyrot, but her regime conformed to the conventions of the time and he went along with it - or at least did not oppose it.

Anyway, it would have been no use arguing with my mother about religion. Her religious views were to her the Laws of the Medes and Persians - unalterable. She was not, however, given to a great parade of her deeply held religious convictions. We did not, for instance, have family morning prayers, although she said her own prayers morning and evening in her bedroom. In the schoolroom we gabbled grace before and after meals, but I think it unlikely that she said grace in the dining room. There were no other daily religious observances, no special Lenten Bible-readings or anything like that. But for all that, my mother, who was not given to any sort of intellectual enquiry, was a convinced religious fundamentalist, and that was the solid, rock-strong foundation of her whole life. To her, every word of the Bible was factually true, and was not to be questioned.

The Bible said: 'Remember that thou keep holy the Sabbath-day'; and keep it holy we jolly well must; but there was nothing jolly about my mother's view of holiness. It was stern, Old Testament stuff – no laughing in Church, and not much at all on Sunday. My mother's God was the tyrannical old Jehovah. He did not laugh. You were lucky if he wasn't frowning. Such a view of the Christian religion was perhaps hardly surprising since the Scriptures are singularly short on any encouragement to mirthful laughter. My mother was not like that herself, being a sweet person who laughed a lot. But that was the religion she had imbibed, and it was not to be questioned.

There either was no Sunday school in Athlone or, if there was one, we did not go to it. From an early age, we went to church. The route to church was one of the pleasantest parts of Sunday. We used to walk to St Mary's Church of Ireland church in the middle of Athlone. To

The Ascendancy was horse-drawn

96

get there we did not follow the road, but took a short cut across the tennis club which was at the back of the churchyard. What made it so pleasant was that on our side of the tennis club there was a high wall. To cross it, we had to climb up and down wooden steps, not much more than a ladder, which was a mild adventure, and fun.

The service we attended was Matins. We sat in the gallery, or at the back of the church. Our parents, and my grandmother and my aunts, sat in their own pews in the nave. The parson was Dean Verschoyle-Campbell, who had conducted my parents' marriage service. If there were hymns we knew – and we gradually got to know many of them – that was all right. The rest was unutterably tedious. Relief came when we were taken out before the sermon, and back, joyfully, over the tennis club wall, and home.

My parents used to play tennis at the club, and there was an occasion when they came back from tennis and told us that one of the Verschoyle-Campbell sons – Willie, I think it was – had just come home from service in India and had brought a mongoose. I was enormously interested, being familiar with Kipling's Rikki-Tikki-Tavi, but I do not recall that I ever saw the mongoose.

Occasionally, we crossed the river and went to church in St Peter's church near the barracks. It must have been used as the garrison church for Anglican soldiers as it was always full of soldiers in uniform. At that time, Sunday church parade was compulsory for soldiers.

There was one way in which Sunday was better than weekdays. The food was more palatable. At lunch there was, as I have mentioned, a roast joint. That was traditional. And at tea there was cake for the only day in the week, even though it was the dry 'missionary cake'.

In passing, it should be recorded that the opportunity presented by Fridays to underline the supposedly beneficial consequences for young children of strict and disagreeable spiritual – and corporeal – observances, was not neglected. Friday was deliberately invested with a gloomy atmosphere, which it has never quite lost for me. Penitential fare was the order of the day, and the lunch-time menu was predictable – one of those lumps of boiled cod, salted hot-water gravy, bicycle tyre wrapping skin and all.

On Sundays we had a 'Scripture' lesson from Miss Hatton. Later on, at school, the subject was dignified by the title 'Divinity'. I think we must have had Scripture lessons during the week as well.

I loved the Bible and Bible stories. I came to know great chunks of it by heart. With a good Irish memory and the absorbent mind of a young child, some of it, once heard, was quite unforgettable. Who could ever forget a phrase such as: 'And David lamented with this lamentation over Saul and Jonathan his son.' I would die happy to have written it. I live uplifted by having such phrases in my mind. In the New English Bible, that phrase has been changed to: 'David made this lament over Saul and Jonathan his son.' How could anyone have been so insensitive as to commit such a literary crime? And it does nothing to make the passage more intelligible.

In departing from the Authorised Version of the Bible and the 1662 Prayer Book, the Church is denying future generations of young people sources of magical English such as will never be written again. The Church's plea is the greater intelligibility of modern English. Of course, sixteenth and seventeenth century English is not so easily understood. But even as a six-year-old child, I was captivated by the magic of the language though I had no idea at the time what it was about it that so appealed to me.

It is fortunate that the works of Shakespeare were not in the custody of some body of similar reformers. They might have reduced them to the language of a television soap opera, and for the same reason - deliberately to vulgarise it in order to widen the readership.

Even at a very early age, I found some of the Bible incredible. A strong practical sense caused me to question some things. I did not believe that Jonah could have remained alive inside the whale, and I had heard somewhere that whales have very small throats, so I doubted that Jonah could have been swallowed.

Likewise, I knew that Shadrach, Meshach and Abed-nego - I loved their names - could not have lived in the burning fiery furnace. I knew enough about fires to know that even if one put a single finger too near the flame, the result was excruciatingly painful.

I enjoyed these sorts of Bible stories, but they took on the form in my understanding of hallowed fairy-tales: like 'Tom Thumb' or 'Jack and the Beanstalk', but sanctified.

Then there was the story of Lazarus and 'Dives', the rich man. This was represented to me as a cautionary tale.

Dives was labelled a 'baddie'. Except to be rich and prosperous, however, he seemed to me to have done nothing wrong. But, for that, he was sent to hell and tormented in the flames. I was not to be like him, or I would suffer the same fate. I did not find him very interesting. As a villain, he was altogether too colourless and unromantic. Moreover, I did not believe he was in hell fire, for the same reason that I discounted the burning fiery furnace story. I knew he couldn't live in the flames. In fact, I was not frightened of hell because I did not believe in it as a place to which anyone could go without being immediately shrivelled up. I doubt that I was conscious of the paradox that, whereas I was to look upon Dives as a baddie, in real life I was taught to respect the rich and prosperous, and to be on my best behaviour when we visited their large houses.

Lazarus I found a much more dramatic figure. I was to regard him as a 'goodie', but I was quite clear in my mind that, if that was goodness, it was not for me, and I would rather risk the consequences of staying bad the way I was – particularly as I was not frightened of hell. I just was not going to sit in someone's gateway, covered in sores and rags and fleas, and be licked by every passing dog, with nothing to eat except crumbs dropped from people's tables.

So, although one half of the cautionary tale was a powerful image, I fear it benefited me little.

Other lovely images remained vividly in my mind: a crazy-looking Elisha being mocked by the children, 'Go up, thou bald-head,' and their fearful punishment when he turned the she-bears on them. The palms of Jezebel's hands – they were blue in my image – after the dogs had eaten her. Poor Ruth: 'Whither thou goest, I will go.' The child Samuel, hearing the voice of the Lord in the dark of the night-watches, running to the bed of Eli the priest, and saying: 'Here am I; for thou calledst me,' and being told, in effect, not to be silly, but to go back to bed like a good boy. Paul, and the blinding light on the road to Damascus. I could see the road, hot and dusty and lined with palm trees, and hear the voice, 'Saul, Saul, why persecutest thou me?'

Or as a centurion saying to one, 'Go, and he goeth; and to another, Come, and he cometh.'

And dozens of other marvellous and unforgettable mental images. I think Miss Hatton must have had a remarkable talent for picking out bits of the Bible that would appeal to a child's imagination, and stick in the mind.

That my thinking was not uncritical, for instance on the existence of hell, as a child of five to seven years of age, may seem curious. But all this can be precisely dated because it all occurred before we left Athlone, when I was seven years old, in the summer of 1915, owing to the circumstances of World War One. I suppose that if one child can play a piano concerto at the age of five years, another may be allowed reasonably advanced views on a subject that catches his imagination. I was not, however, a precocious child, or especially clever. I just think Miss Hatton was a very good teacher. I had a great deal of her time, I was an interested pupil, and I suppose she opened my mind at an early age. It may seem curious to say so of so young a child, but I think that in all things except religion she taught me to be a critical and, if necessary, an unconventional thinker: not to take things for granted, but to think them out for myself. The Bible itself confirmed this attitude. 'Prove all things. Hold fast that which is good.'

To think thus critically is something I could never have learnt from my mother. She did not think. She did not reason. She lived safely by her rigid code of rules, clichés and conventions which served her very well. But for all that, I wonder whether Miss Hatton's enquiring mind had formulated views on the Bible and the Scriptures which she kept to herself. She must have been a contemplative person. She must have spotted that I was puzzled; and I dare say she would have liked and been able, albeit with great care and circumspection, to help me. But with my mother's views what they were, Miss Hatton cannot have been other than wise enough to realise that even the least whisper of any departure from strict orthodoxy just was not acceptable. My mother said I asked more questions as a boy than anyone she had ever known. I wonder if I was usually satisfied with the answers I received. Later on, for instance, when I learnt the Apostle's Creed, my imagination was fired by 'The resurrection of the body', and my mind turned vividly to what would happen at Cornamagh cemetery whither all my funerals went, and I asked my mother about it:

'Will all the people come out of the graves?'

'Yes.'

'Who will un-dig the graves?'

'No one. They will just open up.'

'Who will undo the coffins?'

'No one. The people will just come out.'

'What clothes will they wear?'

'They will have to be provided with clothes.'

'Will they wear the clothes they wore when they died if it was two hundred years ago, or will they wear today's clothes?'

'I don't know. I suppose today's clothes.'

'Will babies come out?'

'Yes.'

'Who will look after them?'

'I suppose their mothers.'

'But what if their mothers went to America and died there?'

'I don't know. Someone will look after them.'

'Will babies grow up in Heaven?'

'I suppose so.'

'Will other people grow old there?'

'I don't think so. Oh! You do ask an awful lot of questions, don't you?'

Miss Hatton was better at training the minds of young children than at warming their hearts.

I never again had a teacher to whom I responded so easily and so completely as I did to Miss Hatton until years later when in India I recruited the services of a slightly dotty old Indian bazaar schoolmaster to teach me Hindustani. Throughout my school career, I think I mostly taught myself. I was quite a good learner, but did not respond well to being taught. It was not that I was at all rebellious, but rather that I have to go on my own, perhaps rather slow, pace. I have the mentality of a boa-constrictor's digestion - slow, but quite capacious.

Part of my religious instruction was taken in hand by my mother.

It was she who taught me the Lord's Prayer, and she also made me learn the Catechism and the Ten Commandments, and I had them all word perfect by the time I was six. Much of it I did not understand, as was doubtless the case with my mother herself. The meaning, however, was the least important part of it to her. What mattered was submitting to a stern piece of religious discipline.

Some splendid passages did excite my imagination. 'To renounce the devil and all his works,' in the Catechism. That was a grand, resounding phrase. It has vanished from the new church services. The church has got rid of the devil, because people just will not go on believing in him and his hellfires. As little more than an infant, I had anticipated the church, in this respect, by half a century.

'Graven images the likeness of anything that is in heaven above, or in the earth beneath, or in the water under the earth.' That provided an exciting stimulus for mental imagery, as did 'the stranger within thy gates,' and the 'manservant, the maidservant, the ox and the ass'.

That 'the Lord did not hold him guiltless' for 'taking His name in vain,' was rather alarming when, even at that tender age, I was conscious that some people were given to a good deal of swearing. I used to look suspiciously and anxiously at the cook to assure myself that she was still all right if, at the moment the milk boiled over, she emitted even such an innocent imprecation as, 'Oh! Lord!' But she escaped. I supposed that somehow that did not count as 'in vain'. At least it saved the rest of the milk. 'Taking His name . . .' it certainly was. Puzzling!

I never heard from my mother that God was love. He was definitely a martinet. He was a jealous God, too, though I wasn't allowed to be jealous myself. Puzzling, again! But one didn't argue. The fear of the Lord was what I was taught. My image of him was of a white-robed, white-bearded old crosspatch, wreathed in clouds, and poised to hurl fire and brimstone and thunderbolts at me. But came the day when that awesome image became somewhat diluted. My older sister Sheelagh threw a Bible at me in a rage. Bibles were usually to hand. I stood in open-mouthed, thunder-struck horror, expecting the inevitable flash of fire and brimstone, or at least that she would become a pillar of salt. Nothing happened. A relief; but also a disappointment. It was an early moment of scriptural doubting.

If those were the religious images I absorbed, I am sure they reflected pretty accurately my mother's variety of fundamentalism, except that hers admitted of no doubts. Intellectual speculation of any sort was to be avoided. That a child of five could not understand the Catechism did not matter. That to learn it was utterly boring and tedious did not matter either. Submission to tedium and boredom could not be other than right, and therefore good, if it conformed with her inviolable rules and conventions.

There was another side to her religious inspiration, a gentler side than its austerities and asperities. All her life there hung in her bedroom two pictures: one, the central Madonna portion of Raphael's beautiful Sistine Madonna; the other, the well-known picture illustrating Isaiah 11:6 – a little child leading the wolf and the lamb, the leopard and the kid, the calf and the young lion.

My father took no part at all in my religious instruction, or any of my teaching.

By the time I was eight years old, I had been filled to the brim with religion. I had been left in no doubt that it was the most important thing in my life. My mother's intention was wholly beneficent – to ensure that I became a good Christian, leading a life strongly founded in the Christian faith which, in the end, would ensure that I was rewarded by a place in Heaven. To that end I must believe unquestioningly whatever I was told to believe. I was taught the scriptures without any explanatory commentary, except that I must accept and believe in them *in toto*, and without any critical examination of their likely validity.

It was a hangover from the days when the Church was a massive temporal power and could, and did, burn you at the stake for the least doubting or questioning of its doctrines, dogmas and scriptures.

My early religious indoctrination did, I believe, strongly underline that it is wrong to be wicked and right to seek to be virtuous, but much of it, the Ten Commandments for instance, was of doubtful relevance to the understanding of a very young child. I was not tempted to commit murder. I did not know what adultery was. Keeping holy the Sabbath-day was a bore that I could not avoid. I did

103

not covet my neighbour's ox, and certainly not his ass.

The south of Ireland, where we lived, was a Roman Catholic country. Only 5% of the population was Protestant. To us there was nothing strange about living in a Roman Catholic country. It was what we had been born into. It was our homeland. It was all we knew. We had no knowledge of any other society with which to compare it. We were used to seeing large numbers of priests in their black clothes, monks in their brown habits and sandals and with small round caps on the back of their heads and always with rosaries, and nuns in their black and white habits, likewise with rosaries.

We knew of no conflict between Roman Catholics and Protestants. Our households were multi-denominational communities who worked and lived together and had a common interest in the well-being of our home. There would be the Master and the Mistress, the children and the governess, Protestants; the cook and the maids, Mary, Bridget, Lizzie, and the man and the boy, Paddy and Michael, Catholics. The only seeming difference was that we, and the governess, went to church on Sunday, and we called the building a church. They, the Catholics, went to Mass, and called their building a chapel. They crossed themselves, and we did not. And they, particularly the women, were apt to say things like: 'Oh! Holy Mary Mother of God, what's happened to the potaters?' which we did not. We were aware that the priests had a specially respected place in society, and I was taught to be particularly polite to them, to touch my cap and call them 'Father'.

There also seemed nothing strange about the fact that almost all the gentry were Protestant, and nearly all the rest of the people Catholic. It just was the way the world was as we knew it.

What did seem strange was when, a little later, we went to England for the first time, all the people there – including, most surprisingly, the servants – seemed to be Protestants; and there appeared to be no priests, monks or nuns.

Much later on, we learnt that the priests preached that all of us Protestants were very wicked for being Protestants, and that we would all go to hell. But no-one seemed to take any notice, or to be at all offended. Nor were the priests any less courteous and polite when we met them.

With that final rumination, I must bring Sunday to a close. And so, come Sunday evening, the Bible would be closed, the Bible stories cease, dear old Hymns Ancient and Modern would be silenced; and it would be up to bed by the ghostly flickering candle light. The gabbled prayers; the agony of the ship-wrecked sailors; and under the bed-clothes while the terrifying witch-laden train roared past – or did it not run on Sundays? And then oblivion till Monday morning and the weekly round once more, and the reality of the hairbrush, the strap and the ruler.

My mention of the conventional households of those days, consisting of family and servants, prompts me to a brief word about that association as I experienced it. It was not a case of oppressor and oppressed. It was a case of a well established and most agreeable unity, strongly underpinned by obligations and affection between all its members, and involving not only lifelong friendships, but even generations of friendship between families. It was particularly beneficial to the children of the family who were in considerable measure brought up by, and influenced by, the servants who inculcated the young with their own high standards. Because it was different from today's conditions, it was not necessarily worse. In particular it provided employment for women when there was little else for many of them to do. Yesterday's parlourmaid may be today's secretary. Is her life, commuting by train and underground to her work, sitting behind a word-processor all day, and returning to a lonely bed-sitter at night, more interesting and more agreeable?

Chapter 10

People

My mother and Miss Hatton have loomed large in the earlier chapters, but I have so far made little mention of other people who were close to me. Of course, we lived in the same house as our father, but we saw little of him. He was a very masculine and undomesticated man, and had no time for small children. Them, like women, he regarded as inferior beings, and they, therefore, were the province of the women. My older sister Sheelagh told me that my father's youngest sister, our Aunt Violet, once said to her that she wondered, when my father was a young man, why he had bothered to get married and have children, because he took absolutely no notice of them. He never sat us on his knee, or read to us, or told us stories.

He and my mother were very hospitable and, in later life, when they lived at our old family home, Killyon Manor, they kept open house, particularly for the family. One day when I was there, I saw my father, then an old man, looking at one of his grandchildren, a baby in a pram. He said to me:

'Do you know? It's a funny thing, but I find these babies and young children much more interesting than I found my own at that age.'

This seeming indifference was not solely due to my father's temperament. It was in part caused by the barrier of women that existed between fathers and their children - mother, nurses, nursemaids, nursery governesses.

Normally, the very young children were available to the father only at prescribed times. They were then liable to be presented to him in ways that were discouraging to the development of an understanding

106

and affectionate relationship. Babies would be thrust into his arms and he would be mocked for not holding them the right way up. That was no way to treat my father. He was not prepared to be mocked by nursemaids. Nor was it any way for a father to get to know his children.

My father was very busy and active at the time and we certainly did not see him daily. He left early for his office, or whatever he might be doing, and I suppose he came home late. I have no recollection of him ever seeing us into bed.

There was an exceptional occasion when he came into the schoolroom one morning, at breakfast time, to show us his new gun. That was typical of him. He always needed an audience, and here was an occasion when his children could meet the need. We could admire his new toy, even if he took no notice of ours.

There were other occasions when I used to be allowed to be with him as I grew a little older. Sometimes he had a bath early in the evening, I suppose if he had been playing tennis or doing something active and, perhaps, if he was going out to dinner. I was allowed in the bathroom while he wallowed, and I used to play with his money and his ring, which were on a shelf. There was a horn there, too, on which I was allowed to try some spluttering blowing.

My father used the horn if he was going to St Mark's by bicycle. He would cycle to Coosan Point and there give a blast or two on the horn. That summoned Johnnie Quigley in his rowing boat to take my father and his bicycle to the further shore of the 'Inner Lake', whence he resumed his bicycle ride to St Mark's.

When I came to learn something of Greek mythology, I always equated Charon with the known scene of operations of Johnnie Quigley rowing northwards across the sometimes stormy peat-brown waters of Lough Ree from Coosan Point. But when Quigley was ferrying my father, it was no cargo of the dead, but a very large and very lively man who kept Johnnie Quigley engrossed with captivating conversation on anything and everything under the sun the whole way across the water. Sitting in a boat with an inescapably captive audience, roaring, if necessary, with his strong voice, even against a drowning gale of wind, my father was in his element.

During those ablutionary sessions in the bathroom at Oldcourt, my father talked endlessly to me, and I grew to love his talk. He was innately loquacious, and laid himself out to be interesting. He had a wonderful memory, stored with a mass of information on all sorts of subjects, and he did not scruple to be plausibly inventive and to embroider to any extent necessary. This was social life, and social intercourse, to him. Social life in his view should, above all, be enjoyable and entertaining, and – though he never said so – clearly from his attitude, not confined by too much pedantic accuracy as to trivial facts.

Other times on which we saw my father were on expeditions when he accompanied us. Then he would be demonstrably in command, shouting orders and instructions and generally making himself felt. A good deal of what mattered went on regardless of him, such as all the preparation of our wonderful Irish picnics; but if, for instance, he undertook to make the picnic fire, there would be as much fuss and noise, involving as many people as possible, collecting sticks, or driftwood from the lake shore, and erecting a few stones as a hearth for the kettle, as there no doubt was getting the Children of Israel out of Egypt, or building Solomon's temple. It was all very good-natured, and reflected my father's natural and constant theatricality. For him 'all the world' was indeed 'a stage', all the time, with himself the leading actor.

He was a larger than life Irishman. He stood 6ft.5½ins. tall, and his height was matched by his strong personality. The fact that he never went to school did not mean that he was particularly lacking in book learning. His wonderful memory was especially noticeable in his knowledge of English literature. He had a great deal of English verse, and not a little prose, by heart. He had enough mathematics to see him through life, and a natural bent for engineering had equipped him with useful practical knowledge which he put to good use in his business life.

He was not an athletic man but he was very hardy, a life-long teetotaller and a small eater. He lived into his eighty-sixth year. Curiously for an Irishman, he did not like horses and never had a bet in his life, but he had great interest in, and much knowledge of, cattle, and kept some all his life. Another outdoor interest was timber, and he gave gratis much good advice on it to friends with timber on their estates. He would have made a good forester.

He was a brilliant shotgun shot, and would walk the bogs of Ireland all day wet to his knees shooting snipe mostly, and flighting duck and golden plover in the evening. He could call the golden plover on a whistle given to him when he was a boy by a poacher. He was also a consistently good cover shot. He would stay out shooting all day until late evening and, wet or dry, he seemed impervious to cold.

He kept dogs, retrievers. They were not allowed into the house but lived in kennels. He had no affection for them and addressed them as brutes. 'Heel! you brute.' They were solely there for shooting, but of course they were our friends when we were children. They for their part exhibited typical and habitual dog loyalty to my father, even to risking their lives for him plunging into dangerously heavy freezing cold flooded rivers to retrieve a duck for him from the far bank. I never thought him a good fisherman, and I saw him doing it often enough as I frequently rowed the boat for him while he fished, but he was usually lucky and caught his fair share.

Money interested him and he had a reasonably successful financial life. He would probably have succeeded as a banker. In dealing with money or business affairs of any kind he was scrupulously concerned to be factual, fair and accurate but, at the same time, in unimportant matters, such as the fish that got away, he had no inhibitions about giving his imagination free rein. Perhaps he had histrionic leanings. As social man he was concerned to be agreeably interesting and to leave a pleasurable impression, rather than to be factual and accurate. He loved talking to women and was a great success with them. He was quite extraordinarily plausible.

He watched his finances on a daily basis, and his final interest in them was typical. All his life he had tended his investments with particular care and, indeed, relish. They were seldom far from his mind and remained a prime interest to him to the very end. On 10 November 1965, my sister Mollie received a telephone call from the staff at the family home, Killyon Manor, to say that they were worried that he seemed to be going downhill rapidly. She immediately drove the forty-five miles from her home in Louth to Killion to see him. She found him in his dressing-gown in his bedroom. He said to her, 'Mollie, I'm dying.' She replied, 'You've been telling me that for the past twenty years.' 'I know,' he said, 'but this time I mean it. Would you be good enough to get me the paper. I want to see how International Nickel are doing.'

Next morning, 11 November 1965, he half woke and said, 'Where am I?' then fell asleep to wake no more. The old loyalist would have been glad to know that he had died on Armistice Day.

After he died his bank manager wrote me a letter deeply regretting the loss of such a long-standing and valued customer. My father

The author's sister, Mollie

claimed himself that he had never had an overdraft. I repeat that he was financially a prudent man.

The other two people most close to me were my sister Sheelagh, eighteen months older than me, and my sister Mollie, eighteen months younger.

Mollie and I never had a quarrel in our lives. We got on together exceedingly well as children and were very close friends. She was a very attractive child, open, outgoing, friendly, light-hearted, kind, devoid of deceit or any meanness; generous indeed, uncomplicated and unselfconscious. She and I played endlessly together, and she was physically active and enjoyed the things I liked such as climbing trees.

She must also have shared at least some of my funeral vigils, for there was a day when, together, we staged a funeral of our own. We found a dead bee. The corpse was prepared for burial; the grave was dug; and the solemn cortege moved off, perhaps to the accompaniment of a hummed Chopin's funeral march, and the internment was duly and ceremonially carried out.

Her laughter and joy in so much that we did together, so many experiences and pranks shared, rings in my ears to this day.

She probably found less interest in Miss Hatton's lessons than I did, but she was that much younger. She learnt to knit and sew and had an abiding interest in the ponies we had.

Mollie and I were, it has always seemed to me, bonded together in some strange way even probably before we could talk. We literally shared a pram. All our lives there was an indissoluble link between us, and, although we might be physically parted for long periods, we nevertheless kept in close contact by letter, writing frequently to each other. There comes a time late in life when, with such a close relationship, one begins to wonder who will go first. I hoped it would be me. For me, the world without Moll was unthinkable. But it was not to be as I wished. In her last days, when she could no longer read, the draft of this book was read to her and she enjoyed it.

Her death left a gaping hole in my life - part of the price of a long life.

Sheelagh could hardly have been more different. Although, much later in life, I had agreeable times with her, she was an ever present trial to Mollie and me when we were small children.

Looking back on the situation in all fairness, it has to be seen that there was an in-built factor in her circumstances which was unfavourable to her. In those times, boy children were regarded in a light that was disproportionately favourable and important. My father, as his father's heir, and having never been to school to have the corners rubbed off him, was, as I have mentioned, spoilt, and was used to having everything his own way. Moreover, being a man of strong character and outstanding personality, and with a quick mind, he was usually well able to ensure that he did have things his own way.

No doubt, therefore, when his first child was on the way, he wished for a son, and looked forward to boasting about it. A daughter was, therefore, doubtless a great disappointment and to have to go about admitting it a painful come-down.

Sheelagh always held that he totally rejected her. She never forgave him and she treated him cruelly much later in life when she had taken to the bottle and he was an old and frail man.

The next child was a son - me - and I, no doubt, on that account received particular attention - enough, it must be supposed, to arouse Sheelagh's jealousy of me. Then, when Mollie arrived after me, I doubtless felt protective to my smaller and younger sister and therefore closer to her than to Sheelagh.

Here then was a triangular situation containing the ingredients of friction. But there was more to it than that.

Sheelagh was highly introverted. Even as a small child, she spent much time day-dreaming and would not be disturbed. And she had disquieting fancies and fantasies. She felt a resentment against the world that she had not been born a princess. Later on, at school, she got enormous satisfaction out of acting the part of grand and noble ladies in school theatricals. She would never join Mollie and me in our games, and was actively disagreeable to us.

Although it is exceptionally hard to pinpoint these things, it must be possible that in this day and age, she would have been judged, as a child, to be at least slightly psychologically disturbed. She was quite successful in some things she did in life. For instance, she joined the

WRNS during World War II, and rose to the rank of 1st Officer, but she was always somewhat eccentric; and, sadly, although an exceptionally healthy person, she died before her time of alcoholism, after she, and all those family members close to her, had had to suffer for years the awful consequences of that dreadful malady from which none of us was able to save her.

While we were at Oldcourt, Athlone, Sheelagh got diphtheria. I think she must have been very ill. It was a wonder that neither Mollie nor I, nor any other member of the household, caught it, and that Sheelagh recovered. Perhaps the wonderful Dr Dobbs was able to insist on the maximum care and hygiene that could be managed. The following extract from a local newspaper of about that time – June 1914 – gives some indication of the health hazards:

Vital Irish Figures
The following statistics are taken from the quarterly return to April, 1914, of the Register General:
59 deaths from enteric, 8 from typhus. Deaths from measles 223, an annual rate of 20 per 1,000. Mortality from scarlet fever 138; from whooping cough 189; from diphtheria 93. The 215 deaths from diarrhoea and enteritis include 176 under two years old. Tuberculosis deaths 2,396. 4,723 deaths were uncertified.

It must seem curious that no cancer deaths were recorded. Perhaps it was seldom diagnosed in those days. A frequent cause of death was 'wasting disease'.

It is to be supposed that statistics for the rest of the British Isles, and indeed for western Europe, would have shown similar trends everywhere. Preventive medicine had not advanced very far, and, perhaps even more important, wonder cures like sulfonamides and antibiotics had not yet been developed.

Today I think that there would be no deaths in the British Isles from any of those causes. We no longer live with the constant shadow of death hanging over us as it seemed to do in those days.

One family story of an early death which moved me when I first heard it when I was very young and which, indeed, touches me still, is a late eighteenth century story of a distant Boothby cousin.

In the village of Ashbourne in Derbyshire there is a truly magnificent church with an immensely high spire – 215 feet. The Boothby family occupied Ashbourne Hall, and the north transept of the church is called the 'Boothby Chapel'.

Among the tombs in the Boothby Chapel is one small work of genius, the beautiful monument lovingly and tenderly carved in pure white Carrara marble, the most notable work of the celebrated eighteenth century sculptor, Thomas Banks. It commemorates Penelope Boothby, only child of Sir Brooke Boothby, 7th. Baronet, and of his wife Susannah. It is of a sleeping child in her night-wear. She lies on her right side, her bare arms folded on her pillow, her cheek resting on her hands. The folds of the beautifully draped night-gown, spread out across the couch-like bed down to her ankles, are a miracle of stone carving. Her small bare feet, relaxed and crossed one upon the other, complete the magic of a work of such affectingly delicate beauty that it speaks for all time the innocence of the last sleep of a loved child.

Tragedy was heaped upon tragedy. An only child, not yet six years old, she was a child so beautiful that Sir Joshua Reynolds chose to paint her, aged three, wearing his own grandmother's mob cap, in his lovely picture 'Simplicity', which in turn, was to be the inspiration for Sir John Millais' no less celebrated picture, 'Cherry Ripe'. So clever was she that the inscription round her tomb is in the four languages of which she already had some knowledge. And – final calamity of all – tradition has it that her mother was so affected by the hopeless tragedy of her loss that, leaving her husband, she fled from the graveside never to return to Ashbourne.

And there is yet more. The various inscriptions round the tomb in English, Latin, French and Italian, are from the greatest word-spinners of all time – adaptions from the Book of Job, a line from Dante, another specially composed by Edmund Burke. The family tribute reads:

To Penelope, only child of Sir Brooke Boothby and Dame Susannah Boothby, born April 11th, 1785: died March 13th,

1791. She was in form and intellect most exquisite. The unfortunate parents ventured their all on this frail bark, and the wreck was total.

No-one who has seen this moving memorial can be surprised to learn that the tender-hearted and motherly Queen Charlotte, when she saw the carving of the sleeping child on exhibition at the Royal Academy, burst into tears.

Here, then, in exquisite miniature, tucked away in the quiet obscurity of rural England, is a coming together of infant genius, parental love, heart-searing tragedy and a feather-weight touch of great art and literature, which make it certain that a loved child of the family Boothby will for ever be remembered, and which surely must bring home to us most poignantly that those days of dreadful child mortality were not by all – probably not by many – accepted with indifference.

There was another family tragedy. Not long before I was born, in one branch of my mother's family, three children, two sisters and a brother, all died together on the same day in what was said to be a pneumonia epidemic.

Of the people who were close to us when we were young, I have particularly strong recollections of Johnnie Duffy and his wife Maggy. He was the boatman whom my father and my Aunt Violet shared: a wonderful sailor, always dressed in a blue jersey and yachting cap.

Maggie used at times to come and help out in the house. She was a well-furnished, motherly person, but had no children of her own, so gave us a full share of her over-brimming affection. She was a good cook, and a visit from her meant a legacy of something much better than the 'missionary cake'. It so happened that when she died I was home on leave from service in India. I went to her funeral in the great St Mary's Roman Catholic chapel in Athlone. Poor Johnnie was there in his blue sailor's jersey and yachting cap. I think they must have been the only clothes he owned.

The gardener at Oldcourt was quite a young man – a bachelor – Paddy Wheatley. He was a particular friend and confidante to Mollie and me, and was a great hand at doing, or helping us with, practical things needing lots of string or wood, or hammer and nails.

At the beginning of World War I in 1914, Paddy joined the British Army, perhaps in an Irish regiment, and went to France. He was terribly wounded and almost wholly incapacitated, and was discharged from the Army.

A house was found for him in the stable yard at Killyon Manor. He did not marry, but lived there well looked-after during the few years that remained to him after the war until, most regrettably, he at last succumbed to his wounds. I was a somewhat older boy by then, and I remember very clearly how strongly I felt that a really good soul had gone out of my life.

There were regular, if not very frequent, visitors to Oldcourt of a kind who would seem strange indeed today. Their place was on the piece of gravel in front of the hall-door that my father called 'the sweep'.

One was the knife grinder. He came pushing a little machine on wheels, and he was given all the knives to sharpen, for which he used a dark chocolate-brown powder. His machine was a pedal grinding mill. He worked the pedal with his foot to set the works in motion and fed the knife blades into a slot with his hands. Stainless steel had not been invented. The steel knives of those days rusted and had to be regularly sharpened.

Somewhat similarly equipped with a pedal mill of a different sort, also pushed on wheels, was another itinerant artisan, the china mender. Broken china was stored up for his visits. People were very thrifty and did not throw even broken things away. The china mender would stick the bits of china together with a white paste that would dry hard. That would not hold together without reinforcement, so he would also put a number of transverse metal stitches across each jointed crack. It was in that metal stitching that his principal skill lay. Some of the china, particularly things like vegetable dish lids which came to the nursery table, had been thus stitched.

Another occasional visitor with a hand-pushed, and this time hand-worked, machine was the organ grinder. Organ-grinders were always Italians and we loved them. We loved the music from the barrel-organ but, most of all, we loved the monkey. There was always a little monkey dressed in quaint clothes sitting on the top of the barrel-organ, which held out a hat for money.

Then sometimes there would arrive a man leading a bear on a chain. The bear was made to get up on its hind legs and dance. We did not like that so much. We had an idea that the bears were trained cruelly and I think we were a bit frightened of them.

From time to time sailors who had been to Russia, Canada or elsewhere in the Arctic would come along selling furs. We had a splendid wolf-skin rug backed with green baize cloth made from such furs, which was used as a motoring rug. Motoring was a cold business in open motorcars with no heaters.

There was one lot of such itinerant callers whom I greatly disliked – the 'Wran Boys'. Wran is how some of the Irish pronounce 'Wren'. On St Stephen's Day – Boxing Day – they used to turn up. They were youths in their 'teens. Their faces were smeared black with the burnt ends of corks and they had battered hats on their heads. They intoned a little ditty:

> The Wran, the Wran,
> The king of all birds,
> St Stephen's Day,
> Was caught in the furze.

I was told that they caught wrens and killed them, and I thought that horrible.

When they had danced up and down for a short time, intoning their ditty, they would hold out their hats for money and would be given a little. In retrospect, I do not suppose they wasted much time trying to catch elusive wrens in very uncomfortable thickets of furze bushes, but more wisely used their time going from house to house holding out their hats.

Ancient conventions of Irish hospitality decreed that the knife grinder and china mender who performed a service for us were given food, and tea to drink. The others would not have been looking for it. Beggars, however, were always given food and tea if they wanted it, but not money, which it was supposed they would spend on liquor.

117

Of course there were other visitors – my father's and mother's friends. Some of them were the local Irish families, others officers from the garrison and their wives. We had no tennis court, so I suppose they came mostly for a gossip over tea, or perhaps after tennis from the tennis club. Sometimes they came to dinner, but that was past our bed-time. Indeed, my Aunt Blossie's diary reveals that it was a time of constant, casual and unplanned social life. As there were no house telephones, it was not easy to make short-term social arrangements. Instead, people were endlessly dropping in on each other unannounced for lunch, tea or dinner, and might then stay the night. I suppose our house was no exception, particularly as my father loved company and both my parents were so welcoming.

There was an evening when some guests were coming to dinner. Mollie and I overheard that they were going to play a game called 'bridge'. We longed to know how it was played because we were avid games players ourselves.

It was to be played in the drawing-room. We knew, with regret, that we could not get down there from our bedroom to peep in and watch, so we had to use our imaginations.

We supposed that there really was only one way it could be played. Two arm-chairs would be put fairly close together, but leaving an adequate passage in between. One grown-up would then stretch himself or herself across the gap by lying with legs on the arm of one chair, and shoulders on the arm of the other. That would make the bridge. The other grown-ups would first crawl under it, and then come back over the top. We tried it with two chairs in the school room, and found it quite diverting.

There were no other children whom we knew well. We used to go to formal Christmas and birthday parties, but might not see the other children again for a year. I remember three boys whom I knew, but not well enough to become close friends with them.

There was one occasion on which I used to meet quite a lot of children, but seemingly did not get to know any of them particularly well. That was at a weekly physical training session in the garrison gymnasium, where an army sergeant instructed us in physical exercises. I particularly enjoyed the wall-bars and Swedish clubs. Dumb-bells I thought tedious. I do not remember children coming to tea, or us going out to tea with others. In the winter, I used to meet boys out of the town, casually, when sliding on the ice which formed on flood water on the Fair Ground opposite our house. I enjoyed that, but it did not lead to friendships.

There were probably a number of reasons why we did not have close friendships with other children. Transporting small children about before the days of the motor car was much less easy than it now is, though my Aunt Blossie's diary suggests that my mother did from time to time have children's tea parties for us. But the root cause probably was that, as we saw it, we neither needed nor wanted to be bothered much with other children. We three children and Miss Hatton, with my mother on the periphery, made a self-contained unit and within it Mollie and I were wholly satisfied with each other, and probably preferred not to share our toys, our time, or our mutual company with outsiders.

A few 'grown-ups' who were especially close friends of my parents were a part of the background to our lives, and we knew them well. Then there were our relations: my grandmother, and my aunts in particular.

I owe it to my Aunt Rachel that I ceased to be called Sonny. I well remember the occasion of my re-christening. I was summoned to appear before my mother and Aunt Rachel. I was told that I was about to be involved in a very serious occasion. Aunt Rachel said she could no longer tolerate me being called Sonny, and my father and mother had agreed that my name should be changed. I was told I had three Christian names, and I could choose to be called by any one of them; or, added my mother, I could be called 'Bill'. I opted for that, and have regretted it ever since. I am devoid of a name with which to sign myself on formal or semi-formal occasions. Children should not be saddled with diminutives and nick-names. Comes the day when they are invited to dinner by a cabinet minister and have no acceptable name with which to sign themselves when writing to thank his wife – and many other occasions when they will be no less embarrassed. I have asserted myself to see that my children were not burdened with that handicap.

Aunt Rachel and her husband, Captain Hugh Dwyer, had no children of their own which perhaps caused them to take a special interest in us. Hugh Dwyer was Rachel's first cousin and therefore our cousin, and so was truly related to us. He was a convivial and entertaining man, and I think he enjoyed having fun with children. There was a particular occasion; perhaps it was Christmas-time, 1914. He had bought a box of conjuring tricks and learnt to do them. He and Aunt Rachel brought them to our home and he kept us spellbound with his wizardry. We sat with him in the drawing-room at Oldcourt for this performance.

One of his tricks involved an object which he showed us and which then disappeared. We looked for it, but it was not to be found. Then he said to me: 'The left hand pocket of my overcoat, hanging in the hall, has magic properties. I wonder could it have got in there?' Off I darted to search for it, and there it was, sure enough. I returned with it in wonderment and excitement, and can see now his cherubic face beaming with pleasure and goodwill.

He later fought in the Mesopotamian campaign in World War I, became very ill and was invalided out of the service. He grew more and more eccentric, but remained a most engaging, congenial, kindly, good-natured and well-intentioned companion.

They were times of social rivalry among a committed socialite element in society, particularly noticeable in Irish families with strong English connections, who were apt to share the money values of upper-class Victorian England. There was one family in particular, who lived close to Athlone, who set out to take the lead in local society. Certainly, in my young eyes, they succeeded in cutting a dash that seemed to me to put people like us in the shade. They went about in spanking equipages which made our poor old pony trap look shabby in the extreme. They dressed richly and smartly, and the women wore extravagant and fashionable clothes – we were only just out of the Edwardian era. They lived in a fine house, and there was much talk of their lavish life-style. They were present in striking evidence on every social and public occasion. My father was derisory about them. He thought them absurd and said, moreover, 'They're living on tick, and they're going to go bust,' and they did, in a welter of bottles.

My father and mother, and my aunts, were not competitive socialites. In their own eyes they had no need to be. My father's family, being very ancient Irish landowners, felt no social insecurity. My mother felt likewise, coming as she did of an ancient English landed family, her branch of which had been Irish landowners for several centuries. Furthermore, my mother was too simple and innocent and nice even to be aware of the social in-fighting which was a part – though perhaps only a small part – of local life, and too thrifty to waste money on fripperies. My father furthermore had had the experience of seeing his own father living extravagantly – as he thought – in order to keep up appearances. My father thus regarded solvency as very much more important than appearances.

People who should have been a large influence in our young lives but, as I have recorded, were not, were my mother's parents and her brother and three sisters. Later in life I came to know my Biddulph aunts. They were all, each in her own way, interesting people, and I liked them all, but nothing could make up for the lost years of childhood. They never meant as much to me, and I could never be as close to them, as I was to my lovely Magan aunts. The blight of our maternal grandmother's wickedly hostile attitude towards our family undoubtedly cast a shadow over our young lives.

Chapter 11

World War One: The Beginning

I do not know what time the news reached Athlone on 4 August, 1914, that we were at war with Germany, or by what means it came - telegraph, I suppose, to the Post Office; it would be another twenty years before radio broadcasting would become fairly common - but my father heard it in time to catch the night boat to Holyhead that night and to present himself to the War Office next morning to be granted Emergency Commission No.13 in the British Army.

He returned to Ireland and joined a unit at Kingsbridge, on the west edge of Dublin city, for training, and was soon sent to France. But shortly after that, a family event took place.

On the night of 10 November 1914, not long after we had gone to bed, there was a lot of bustle and scurrying up and downstairs, talking in hushed tones and a variety of other noises and movements. Perhaps we went to sleep, and it may not have been until next day that we were informed that we had a baby sister - Maureen. Her birth reminds me of an Irish story.

An Irish woman wrote to her son who was working in England:

Dear Pat. I am sure you will be delighted to hear that your sister Mary had a baby last night. I haven't seen it yet so don't know whether you are an uncle or an aunt.'

Life for us after Maureen's birth fell unusually flat, as we were told that we could not see our mother because she was ill. We were cut off from her for some days and felt deprived.

Then, one day, a messenger boy arrived at the front door. I

The girls collecting for the Red Cross, myself collecting for Belgian refugees

happened to intercept him before anyone else was aware that he was there. He had come from the chemist and had brought a bottle of medicine for my mother. I could not resist the temptation and the chance this gave me to see her so, although I knew I was being disobedient and might suffer for it, I took it up to her room.

She was lying on her back in bed, awake, but doing nothing. She took no notice of me. I tiptoed across the room and put the medicine on her dressing table. I tiptoed back to the door and looked at her but she still took no notice of me. I was very puzzled, but quietly went out and shut the door.

Having, in the nature of things, never myself suffered post-natal conditions, I cannot guess what was wrong with her. She was a person of the greatest equanimity, never particularly elated, nor ever depressed. But this time she must have been fairly seriously ill. Today she would have been in hospital.

My father's precipitate dash to get into the armed forces of the Crown was typical of the burning loyalty of the Anglo-Irish gentry. Without even an hour's hesitation, he left his wife and three children (and one on the way), his home, his work and his money-making activities. He was succeeding in his business ventures and doing well financially, and must have suffered a substantial loss of income.

We all became highly conscious of the war situation. A special home-made soldier's uniform was made for me, a far from smart affair but a great improvement on the Little Lord Fauntleroy velvet suit. We had other special uniforms, and a collecting box with the Belgian national colours on it with which we went collecting for the Belgian refugees – it was Germany's invasion of Belgium that brought Britain into the war. In addition, we had a uniform with large red crosses on it in which we collected for the Red Cross.

There was much movement of troops, and much activity in connection with the military and the Athlone barracks. One of the activities that affected me was that many women volunteered for nursing courses. In particular they had to learn the correct way to bandage injured limbs. I was told that I was to pretend to be a wounded soldier and let myself be bandaged. However, I had very proper ideas of the extent to which I was prepared to allow myself to be exposed to strange young ladies. They took off my jacket, rolled up my sleeves, and bandaged my hands and arms. They then wanted to remove my shirt, but I was adamant in my refusal to allow it. They then tried to set about my nether regions, but I would have none of it. I would not even let them take my stockings off. If they wanted to bandage my legs, they must do it with my stockings on. It was wartime, and I was quite prepared to fight for my own rights and sense of decency.

Soon we began to experience the grimmer side of war. Not long after war had been declared, the military laid on a gymkhana to which we were invited. There was a tug-of-war. Two of those taking part, both captains, one a short portly man, the other a tall thin man, were people we knew. I was told to go and cheer them on, which I did. A few weeks later I was told that they had both gone to France and been killed.

From then on we were to hear frequently of the death of people known to us or to our parents. But I do not recall that I found such news particularly disturbing. I think children are little affected by happenings remote from the immediate vicinity of their lives.

My mother with Mollie, me, Maureen and Sheelagh at Greystones 1915

125

The dreadful consequences of the war were really brought home to me, however, by those spine-chilling military funerals, now more frequent.

My father went to France at the end of October 1914, after less than three months' army service; and in 1915 it was decided that we would go and live temporarily in Greystones, a very nice little town on the sea, on the east coast, some twenty miles south of Dublin. The reason was that forty-eight hours leave was all that was normally given to officers serving in France, which would hardly give my father time to get to Athlone and back, whereas the mail boat from England came to Kingstown – as Dun Laoghaire was then called – only a few miles up the coast from Greystones. It was many years before the time of air services.

I remember only one visit from my father to Greystones, a very short one, I think. Perhaps it was in June 1915, because he gave me a present for my birthday, which is in June. His sisters were there to greet him, and perhaps my grandmother. He arrived in the morning in uniform, went into the drawing-room of our house and told endless stories about the trenches. My Aunt Rachel said she found it hard to believe some of it.

The present he gave me was unusual. It was a cheque – I had never had a cheque before – for £1. I was told I could cash it at the post office, so Miss Hatton and I went there and exchanged it for a real golden sovereign.

I did not much like the house we had, but there were other things about Greystones which I did enjoy. I loved the seashore, so long as I could run about in gym shoes and do what I liked. One of the things I liked was playing leap-frog over some old breakwater posts. Sea bathing from a sandy shore had little appeal for me. The water was cold; it went up my nose; and, neither then nor ever since have I liked sand between my toes.

I joined a Boy Scout group and much enjoyed that. It was brilliant of the early organisers of the scouts to think up the system of badges. It takes some effort and some skill to win them, but not too much, and certainly not a heart-breaking amount of either. So a reasonably diligent scout can give himself the immense satisfaction of decorating himself with a considerable number of imaginatively designed and coloured badges.

I also went to a Sunday School class. I was delighted with the little coloured cards we were given with religious pictures and illuminated texts printed on them.

One Sunday we had the thrilling experience of a talk from a real live missionary from Africa, and he brought with him African artefacts to show us – assegais, strange hats, beads and so on. I suppose his skill was converting people. He converted me. I decided to be a missionary, so that I could get plenty of lion hunting.

From time to time we returned to Athlone for a few weeks or months, and we changed to a much nicer house in Greystones near the beach.

One time while we were in Athlone, my father did manage to visit us very briefly, and not long afterwards he came home again ill, and was at home for some weeks before he was sufficiently recovered to go back to France.

We were in Athlone when the Irish rebellion of Easter 1916, occurred. News of what was happening was confused, and we had feelings of uncertainty and anxiety, but I have one particular and very vivid recollection.

There was much military activity and movement of troops. Troop trains passed through Athlone and some of the ladies, including my mother, and a close friend, Mrs Handcock, set up a 'soup-kitchen' on the platform of the Midland Railway station, the other side of the Shannon. I was taken there to see what was going on.

It was a bright sunny day. What I saw was a train-load of policemen. I asked what was happening to them. I was told they were going to fight the rebels. I asked if any of them would be killed. I was told that a lot of people had already been killed, and more probably would be. I looked at those marvellous big men in their dark green uniforms walking up and down the platform in the sunshine eating sandwiches and drinking mugs of tea or soup, and I was quite horrified to think that some of those very ones I was looking at might in a few days be in a coffin, dead and screwed down and in one of those dreadful hearses, going slowly, with a crowd of mourners, to the grave.

It may be thought that I had funerals on the brain. I suppose in a sense I had, and it was all very private with me; I never talked about it. But ever since, and all through life, I have never been able to come to terms with the fact that death is a perfectly natural part of life. I have always hated its dreadful and absolute finality, the total, impenetrable cut-off from those who have dwelt in the warmth of one's affections.

After the rebellion, we returned to Greystones. I greatly enjoyed the different house we now rented there. It was bigger than the one we had had before. There was a garden between it and the road and, from that road, a small road ran down to the sea, a couple of hundred yards away.

We had nice and interesting neighbours. In the next house to our left, as we faced the sea, lived a kindly, eccentric old fellow who grew tropical plants which I viewed with great wonder.

In the next house to the right were the Cargan family. Mr Cargan was dead. Mrs Cargan, who seemed elderly to me, lived there with her two daughters. She gave me two books, *The Gorilla Hunters*, and *Coral Island*, by R.M. Ballantyne, which were closely associated in my mind with the tropical plants next door.

Agnes, the older of Mrs Cargan's daughters, looked after the house and her mother. She was charming and always most welcoming and kindly to me. One day I had the excitement of successfully helping her to find a precious stone she had lost from a ring. The younger daughter, Eleanor, was a student in Dublin, perhaps at Trinity College, where she went, I think, daily. She was sparkling gaiety personified, and I loved her dearly.

In Greystones, with those neighbours and the sound of the sea ever in my ears, the sun shone for me, except when there were great and awesome storms, one of which washed away the railway that ran on an embankment between us and the shore, twisted the rails as though they were bits of wire, broke up huge slabs of reinforcing concrete as though they were sticks of chalk and added a great wonder and excitement to my life.

One day, after a storm, Mollie and I went beach-combing, and we came across a number of little pinnacles of sand, each an inch or so high, and each with a coin resting on top of it - riches for us; or should it have been treasure trove?

In that happy life, there were clouds and shadows too.

One day I was walking down the little road leading from our house to the beach, when round the corner at the bottom came a light cart with two boys standing in it lashing on the pony which was going full gallop. As it rounded the corner, going much too fast, the cart overturned. The pony went down and the two boys were thrown out. One of them picked himself up. The other lay motionless with his eyes closed. I thought he must be dead. I ran back to the house for help. I do not remember just what happened next, but the mess was cleared up, and the boy taken to hospital.

I kept asking for the next few days how he was. I was told that he was not dead and would soon be all right. Then, one day, I was told he was back at work. I found it hard to believe that someone I had left for dead could be back at work. I asked if I could see him. I was taken to the place where he worked, some little industry I think, where I suppose he was an apprentice, and there he was working away at a bench looking as though nothing had happened to him. I have the

Myself at Greystones, Co. Wicklow, c1915

129

strongest recollection of the feeling of astonishment that overcame me.

Motor vehicles may cause a lot of accidents, but horse-drawn vehicles were not altogether safe. Two or three years earlier than this accident, a member of one of the families who worked at Killyon, Christopher Lacey, was killed by a fall from a cart on the road near the Killyon gates.

It was in that house in Greystones, too, that I came upon my mother weeping over her father's death.

But the darkest imaginable cloud rolled up and blotted the sun from the lives of us children in the summer of 1916. By then Sheelagh was nine and a half years old, and I eight years. Miss Hatton felt that we had passed out of her age group as a nursery governess, and that it was therefore time that she should seek a post elsewhere. She had been our constant companion for almost all of the life that we could remember. With her departure the foundation of our feeling of security would be destroyed. When the news was broken to us we were quite inconsolable. We felt cast off from our moorings and dangerously adrift. We howled for a week before she left, and for another week after she had gone. Not all the howling wolf packs of the far Canadian North ever raised so great a lamentation to the star-lit heavens. I think it probable that I got a much better intellectual start in life from Miss Hatton than I would have got from one of today's nursery schools.

In her place we got a governess who called daily. She was elderly, perhaps retired. Her name was Miss Gower (or Gowers). She was a gentle soul, but did not have a chance with us. We were not prepared to give our trust to a stranger and, to us, an interloper. I fear my education made no progress for the few weeks she was with us before we returned to our home, Oldcourt, at Athlone.

By then we were old enough to have some independence. For instance, I used to walk over to see my grandmother and my aunts at Ardaghcourt, the house that became their home after St Mark's was burnt. It was just beyond the eastern limits of the town of Athlone, and something under a mile from where we lived at Oldcourt. They also took us about with them individually. I was very honoured to be taken by my Aunt Violet to Rathrobin for Uncle Middleton's and Aunt Vera's silver wedding celebrations. No doubt we used also to go on our feet into the town and round about to see people we knew. There was a very active social life in and about Athlone with the British garrison there and, although I no longer remember run of the mill day to day happenings, we, as children of seven to nine years of age, doubtless had our share of it.

In early October 1916, my father, after two years in France, was posted back to England to a staff job in the War Office, and he and my mother decided to take a house in London from which he could conveniently get to work.

So on 11 January 1917, we left Oldcourt, as it was to turn out for ever; and that evening my mother, with her four children and three maids, boarded the mail boat at Kingstown and set sail on our journey to London. For the first of very many times we were about to make that well-worn journey: a rough sea to Holyhead, where the Irish Mail, as the London and North Western Railway express train was known, awaited passengers alongside the dock; then the train journey across Anglesey and the slow rumble through the tubular bridge to the mainland across the Menai Straights; through Wales, and then the four well-known stops which the porters at Holyhead used to sing out while the passengers from the boat were boarding the train – 'Chester, Crewe, Rugby, Willesden'; finally to draw into London at Euston Station, so different then from now, a massive Victorian building, with a fine railway hotel of the period and a splendid, almost ceremonial, archway into the station precincts. At one time a rubber road was laid down under the archway to test the value of rubber for road surfacing against a recordable volume of traffic.

From Euston we went, probably by hansom cab, to our new home, 25 Alexander Place, Bayswater, a narrow up and down house of, I think, four or five stories: all, I dare say, that my parents could get to rent at short notice in wartime; and we children, from being country dwellers in Ireland, had to accommodate our Irish souls to the altogether different life of England's greatest city.

The winter of 1916/17 was exceptionally cold. Not long after we left Athlone, Lough Ree was frozen over, and people cycled on it - a pleasure denied to me by our exodus to England. With the exodus, too, I passed out of a phase of life. I left my childhood behind. I was now a boy.

Chapter 12

Wartime: Preparatory School, 1917-19

Serving in France in 1914-16, in World War I, my father became very friendly with another Wartime Emergency Commissioned Officer, F.E. (Fred) Chappell who, at that time, was a bachelor.

Mr Chappell, as I shall call him here because he was always Mr Chappell to me, was a schoolmaster. He had been an assistant master at a preparatory school in Purley, Surrey, but some years before the war had had the initiative to set up his own school, The Downs, at Purley, Surrey. There my father decided to send me, and there I arrived in late April 1917. I had travelled from London by train with a master and two other boys. From the station we trundled and rumbled up to the school in a horse-drawn cab.

The school was, for those days, a modern house, perhaps late Victorian or Edwardian, and, although it appeared quite a modest building compared with Irish mansions, it must have been fairly commodious as it accommodated the staff and forty-five boys, and there was ample class-room space.

Mr Chappell was, indeed, an enterprising man for, although it was wartime, he had managed to add to the amenities two large, pre-fabricated, wooden army huts, where we had a carpenter's shop, gymnasium, and space for other activities.

My first evening at school has faded from my mind, but I have a clear recollection of the start of the next day. We gathered round the tiled fireplace in a small hall opposite the dining-room door to wait for breakfast, and everyone seemed to be concerned to congratulate a boy who had won a good scholarship. I did not even know what a scholarship was. I recall him as a quiet, gentle person, absorbed in

133

intellectual interests and little given to physical pursuits.

Although I had not been much used to mixing with other boys, I found no difficulty in doing so, and I very soon became a normal member of the community in my dormitory and my class. I never felt home-sick. At times I felt conversationally inadequate, because I had not shared the background and experiences of most of the other boys. None of them was Irish. Some, if not all, of them, particularly if they lived in or within easy reach of London, had been to museums, picture galleries and so on, things of which I had little experience.

When I arrived at The Downs, Mr Chappell was still serving in the Army overseas, and the school was looked after by his second master, Mr Standfast – known as 'Sticky' – who had some disability rendering him unfit for military service. He was an exceedingly nice man, a bachelor at that time.

In the mornings, he timed his arrival at breakfast to coincide exactly with the moment we had filed into the dining-room and reached our chairs. His approach was always heralded by a loud trumpeting on his handkerchief as he came down the stairs. Like himself, the matron, Miss Salmon, was a very charming person. She was kind and motherly but, sadly, left to get married not long after I joined the school.

It was the height of the war. Casualties were heavy. Able-bodied young men were all in the services or doing other essential war work. In consequence, we had no young masters. Instead, we had an unconventional assortment of teachers. Apart from Mr Standfast, who was a good mathematics master, the only one who remained any length of time was Mr Blanchard – a man of about forty years, likewise a bachelor, who may also have had some disability. He too was a good teacher who taught Latin and English subjects, including Divinity. He was a man of somewhat uncertain temperament, given to having favourites, and you never knew whether you were likely to be in or out of favour, but we tamed him: boys are not fools.

Mr Blanchard had one special skill, over which he took much trouble and which I think he enjoyed. He used to read aloud to us at supper time, good adventure stories. He planned each day's reading exactly. He edited the text to cut out anything the least boring, and always ended at a point of cliff-hanging suspense:

'At that moment the door swung slowly open, and a hairy hand . . .'

Bang! Old Blanchard would slam the book shut to cries of, 'Oo'oo!' from us, and we couldn't wait till supper time next evening.

We had a mistress of whom I remember little and, for a time, a rather barmy old baronet who had an enormous collection of pencils of all shapes, sizes and colours, an occasional one of which would be handed out to some boy as a special reward. Why, I do not know, but the baronet did not dwell in the school house but in a partitioned-off cubicle in one of the army huts. Perhaps he snored.

Then, for a time, we had an Indian, a quiet, gentle and conspicuously courteous person. He was to us of particular interest, and was also a great disappointment.

We had got it into our heads that Indians were great jumpers, and when we were told that an Indian was joining the staff we could not wait to see him jump. No sooner had he arrived than we were urging him to come out to the playing field and jump. We could not believe it when we found he could not manage more than three feet. We could do better than that ourselves. But we were not prepared to give up. We felt that somewhere hidden inside him was a seven-foot leap if only we could coax or force it out of him. So, day after day, we urged the poor man to jump, but all to no avail.

At lessons, needless to say, I had no problems with divinity or with elementary mathematics; and history, English and geography I enjoyed. But, having previously had no language lessons, I had difficulty with Latin and French. The wartime dearth of masters left us with no-one to teach us Greek.

Exams for me had something of the pleasurable anticipated excitement of lucky dips. A good short-term memory meant that I could always do some productive mugging-up in advance. Duplicators either did not exist or we did not have one. Exam papers were written by the masters in purple ink. That was transferred to the surface of a tray of special gelatinous substance, from which a sufficient number of copies could be taken by pressing the papers onto it.

Every now and again, Mr Chappell would come back for a few days leave and he always took some classes, no doubt to assure himself that the boys were being adequately taught. He had a friend, a very nice person, who used to visit us when he was there, Lady Blane, widow of Captain Sir Charles Blane, Bt. RN, who had been killed on 31 May 1916 when his battle-cruiser, the *Queen Mary*, had been sunk during the Battle of Jutland, one of the greatest sea battles of all time. The British and German fleets combined totalled 249 ships. We thought, and hoped, because we particularly liked her, that some romance might be brewing between Mr Chappell and Lady Blane, but we were wrong. She lived to a ripe old age but did not marry again.

The Downs was a very civilized place. There was no bullying, no gross misbehaviour, no harshness, and no corporal punishment, because Mr Chappell was wholly opposed to it.

Games were, of course, compulsory, but were there to be enjoyed and not given exaggerated importance. Our groundsman, Archie, was one of those avuncular figures without whom the complement of no prep-school would be complete. He was handy man of all works and all skills, and he cleaned the boots and humped the coals. He got through a prodigious amount of work at a seemingly unvaried leisurely pace. He taught us carpentry and boxing, to dribble a football and shoot at goal, to catch and bowl and bat at cricket.

I had not previously played games like cricket, hockey and football, but took to them readily enough. My début into cricket was spectacular, and took place a day or two after I joined the school.

We assembled on the cricket ground. I had not the faintest notion what it was all about. As I now know, but did not then understand, the other side had been put in to bat, and my side was fielding. We were told to stand in different parts of the field. One boy, all dressed up in pads and large gloves, stood behind the wicket, and I was told to stand behind him and a bit to his right (1st slip), and to try to stop the ball and throw it to him if it came my way. In front of the wicket stood a boy with a bat.

After a few moments of bewildering inaction and suspense, things began to happen. A boy at the other end began running very fast towards the other wicket. When he got there he hurled the ball at the batsman. It hit the bat and flew towards me. I grabbed it and threw it to the wicket-keeper.

There was a great outburst of applause and clapping, and the boy with the bat walked slowly and sadly off the field. My total incomprehension of these proceedings was finally dispelled when it was explained to me that I had caught him out. Is that a record? A clean catch not only off the first ball of the game, but off the very first ball of a never to be very distinguished cricketing career, by someone who had not the least idea what he was doing, or why he was doing it. It has to be understood that there was no television in those days, and not much cricket in rural Ireland, so that I had never before seen a game of cricket. As an Irishman, I find myself at one with whoever it was who said that the English are not a very spiritual people, and therefore invented cricket to give themselves some experience of eternity.

Purley was then a well-to-do outer suburb on the edge of rural country, and The Downs school was on the fringe of the village. A mile or so from the school was a large grass field which contained the Purley Aerodrome. It later became Croydon Airport, and was then abandoned for Northolt and then Heathrow.

The Purley Aerodrome in 1917 was a flying training school for wartime pilots. The principal training aircraft was the AVRO, but there were other aircraft there as well; the BE2 C and later, the Sopwith Pup, the Sopwith Camel and I think others.

The aerodrome consisted of the grass field and a few canvas hangars to house the aircraft, in front of which was an early asphalt apron as a hard standing for the aircraft. The only other conspicuous furnishing was the 'wind sock' to show pilots the direction of the wind. As there were no runways, aircraft could take off or land on the grass, directly into the wind. I was puzzled about the asphalt. The word, as I heard it pronounced, sounded like 'assfelt', and I supposed the area, for some strange reason, to have been laid down with donkey skins.

The first Sunday I was at The Downs, we went for a walk to the aerodrome. We stood near the hangars on a small road, flanked with low trees, which formed one boundary of the airfield, and we watched the aeroplanes with intense interest. They included a couple of AVROs being prepared for take off.

At one moment, I heard an aircraft behind us, and saw one coming in to land right over us. It looked terribly low and, although I knew nothing about flying, I wondered if it was going to clear the trees under which we were standing. It didn't. It hit them above our heads, carried on a few feet, and plunged into the ground just in front of us. The tail came over the nose and the aeroplane buckled into three pieces; the pilot in his leather equipment, flying helmet, field-boots and all, was hanging by his straps from the open cockpit in the centre section. In a moment, the roar of the engine and the crashing of the trees were silenced and gave way to an eerie stillness. Then the men came running from the other aircraft, plunged under the cockpit and pulled out the pilot who had been flying solo. They stood him on his feet, stuck a lighted cigarette in his mouth and, one each side of him, with their arms linked in his, they walked him to the hangars. He was a lucky man. He seemed shaken but unhurt.

But not all were so lucky. There were always aeroplanes in the air, and we loved watching them. They were very slow compared with modern aircraft. I think the AVRO flew at about eighty miles per hour. The later Sopwiths, which were very pretty little aeroplanes, were somewhat faster. By the time the 1st World War ended, no aeroplane had been built that could fly at as much as 150 miles per hour.

In addition to all their other flying drills, the pilots were taught three particular and spectacular stunts. The aeroplane would go up several thousand feet and then go into a vertical nose-dive, would spin all the way down and then pull out into horizontal flight when a few hundred feet from the ground. Sometimes they used to do it right above our playing field.

The second manoeuvre was recovery from a stall. This, too, had to be practised from a certain altitude. The aeroplane's power would be reduced. The aircraft would lose momentum. Its nose would go down, and it would stall out of control. The power had to be restored, control recovered, and the machine flattened out into level flight once more.

The third manoeuvre was looping-the-loop. One day I saw an

AVRO loop-the-loop at a very low altitude. As it reached the top of the loop it stalled and fell backwards. It was too low for recovery, and dropped out of sight behind a hill and some trees – an unforgettably sickening spectacle.

Parachutes were a novelty, and we used to see early parachuting experiments. Sometimes dummies were dropped; sometimes there were live drops. One day I saw a parachute dropped. It became a long white stick, but opened no further, and fell like a stone. I still pray, as I did then, that the body on the end of it was a dummy.

Soon after the war there was an air race called the King's Cup. The course took the aeroplanes exactly over our school, and they flew very low – I would say two or three hundred feet. Most of the aeroplanes at that time were bi-planes, but I have a strong recollection that our interest was focused on a monoplane flown by a famous pioneer pilot, Harry Hawker, who, though British, had been born in Australia.

During the 1st War we had to endure air raids. They were nothing like the scale of the 2nd War, but were, nevertheless, not negligible. Some were by airships – Zeppelins – and some by aeroplanes. They caused a total of some 4,800 casualties, of whom 1,500 were killed. No bombs dropped near our school, but we watched the scanning searchlights every night hoping to see a Zeppelin caught in the beam of one of them; and sometimes there was anti-aircraft fire.

One bright moonlight night, the anti-aircraft fire was so intense in our vicinity that it was decided to vacate the dormitories and take us downstairs into the biggest classroom. The house was, of course, blacked out, and we stood in our dressing-gowns to keep warm, looking out of the windows, but we saw nothing except the searchlight beams. The precaution of taking us into the classroom was not to protect us from a bomb which would have gone right through the building, but to save us from possible large fragments of anti-aircraft shells which might come through the roof. However, nothing happened. Eventually the noise died down, and we were shepherded back to bed.

Next day we learnt that a German pilot had landed his aeroplane on the Purley Aerodrome in the moonlight, taxied across to the canvas hangars, sprayed them with machine-gun fire, and safely taken off again. I have to confess that admiration for this daring exploit rose above our more general patriotic wartime anti-German feelings.

Even though the 1st War air raids were small by comparison with the 2nd War, we were nevertheless conscious all the time of the war and its dangers, and particularly so in July 1918, when the Germans launched their last great offensive and we could distinctly hear the guns booming away in France.

We had one or two model makers in the school who made really beautiful models of the wartime aeroplanes. I would like to think that some of them may have survived to find a place in some museum.

Parents seldom visited the school, perhaps owing to transport difficulties before motor cars became general, and perhaps because the habit of frequent visits had not become usual. I do not think my mother ever visited The Downs. My father came once. He arrived in the evening, stayed the night, and did not leave until after morning break next day.

For morning break there was a glass of milk and some broken biscuits, but we had to pay for the biscuits - a penny a handful, I think. I am not sure why we paid for them - not to get money off us, I am sure; Mr Chappell was not that sort of man. It was more likely an early lesson to teach us that you don't always get something for nothing.

My father was there when the milk and biscuits were being dished out, and I hoped he would offer to pay for everyone's biscuits. He did not disappoint me, and I was very pleased.

Just as parental visits were rare, so were exeats. I think boys were allowed home for one weekend in the term. When the war ended, my parents went back to Ireland where I could not go home for a weekend, because it took too long before the days of passenger aircraft. But on at least two occasions, I stayed with other people. There was a very nice boy in the school who had a withered arm. He had two aunts who lived together in Purley. He, and they, kindly invited me to spend a half-term weekend with them.

On one of the days, we took our lunch out for a picnic. It was a bright, warm, sunny summer's day. We found a corner of a nice field where we sat on the edge of the sweet smelling hay near a barn. While we were having our lunch a great blue-black cloud built up over Purley, and there was a spectacular thunder-storm, but it missed us.

The aunts were exceptionally nice and very jolly, and we had lots of good laughs, even at slightly risqué prep-schoolboy jokes.

Then one of them asked me how old I was. I told her.

'And when is your birthday?'

'Well, as a matter of fact, it happens to be today.'

'Good gracious! Why on earth didn't you tell us?'

There was great rejoicing and bustle. We must hurry home, and there must be a real birthday tea. So we packed up and made for home.

Purley showed all the signs of having been hit by a heavy storm. Although it was mid-June, the roads were strewn with green leaves, twigs and pebbles, and water was still foaming down the gutters.

As we rounded a corner near the aunt's house, we saw a fire-engine in the road, and firemen still working on the smoking roof of a house that had been struck by lightning.

At all events, despite the austerities of wartime, a worthy birthday tea was contrived, and I had a lovely week-end. I am sure that the two old girls, just going along with the normal promptings of their cheerful, benevolent good natures, never imagined that they were implanting in a young mind a glowing picture of their own commonsensical goodness and goodwill that would not have lost one iota of its freshness in three-quarters of a century to come.

Hugh Dwyer, the man of the conjuring tricks, who had married his first cousin, my aunt Rachel Magan, had an older brother, also in the British army, Lt. Colonel Jim Dwyer, DSO, who died in Calais as a result of his war service in February 1919, almost two years after I went to The Downs. He had married another cousin, the sweet and captivating Marie Hussey-Walsh. She had no children and, after Jim's death, settled in a small house in London, where she was good enough to invite me for a half-term weekend.

From the moment she met me at the station, she treated me with a relaxed friendliness that someone with a lifetime's experience of handling boys might have envied. She made me, so to speak, her partner for the weekend. We did not do anything very much, or anything that might be considered very exciting – except one thing: a surprise at the very end. She just asked me, as she went along, to help her in the things she was doing, but we never stopped doing them. I gave a hand in the kitchen and with other household chores. We made a cake and I licked the bowls. There was a continuous stream of ordinary but pleasant and satisfying tasks.

She didn't boss me. She treated me as her equal, and just did me the honour of entrusting me with the responsibility of sharing in what she was doing.

At one moment she called to me from the dining-room, and said there was a mouse there, and could I do anything about it. Could I not? Boys are nippy and natural hunters; I was after that mouse like a terrier and by an extraordinary piece of luck caught it. I jammed it against the wainscot with my foot, and grabbed it with my hand.

I was immensely pleased, and particularly because I earned warm commendation from Marie. I said it was an awful fluke, which it was, but she wouldn't have it. She said I was better than any mousetrap. I was having the sort of experience for which males are prepared to lay down their lives – to be told by the lovely Marie that I was better than a mousetrap. What more could any man ask? Such compliments were a total novelty to one more accustomed, as I was, to 'could do better'.

She had to do some visiting; she took me with her and introduced me to her friends in a grown-up sort of way as 'my cousin'. I had never been so honoured. To receive what almost amounted to a title, and in public, and to be elevated thus to her own grown-up level. 'Cousin!' That was indeed a word and a distinction to be savoured. I felt inches taller.

On the last evening she sprang her surprise. She said that because I had been so helpful, she would like to give me a present. The son of some friends of hers who lived nearby, had, at seventeen years of age, grown out of his air-rifle. It was going cheap. She would like to give it to me. We couldn't wait to call on the friends, and I returned to her house, my senses almost numbed with the wholly unexpected experience of finding myself the unimagined owner of such a trophy.

And so it wasn't just back to 'could do better', and all that. My return to school was triumphant. I became the esteemed object of a quite unwonted regard among my fellows. Of course the rifle was taken into custody, but we were allowed to use it under supervision. We all learnt to shoot with it. And I discovered a curious thing. I found that if, immediately on pulling the trigger, I focused my eyes at a certain distance from the muzzle, I could see the fired pellet in the air and knew whether it was high or low, right or left of the target.

Magan's gun thus became a feature of the life of the school, and something about which to write home.

My Dwyer cousins were Roman Catholics. My great grandfather, George Percy Magan, had married a Roman Catholic, Ellen O'Connor-Henchy. By a family arrangement their sons were brought up Protestants, from one of whom I descend. The daughters were brought up Catholic, from one of whom the Dwyer brothers descended. Marie herself was a Catholic, although her mother had been Protestant. Thus, when she died at over eighty years of age Marie's funeral was held at the great London Catholic church, the Brompton Oratory. During the service, I recalled the mouse and the air-gun, and I thought how nice it would be if some, just a few, of 'the loveliest and the best' might remain young and beautiful and live for ever, to go on being an inspiration for good in a world sorely in need of it. Not the least need is in Ireland itself with its perennial religious strife. But within our own family, there was no religious friction or dissension.

The Magans were staunchly Protestant; their cousins, Marie Hussey-Walsh's family, no less staunchly Catholic. Had not their ancestor fought in the Irish Catholic Confederacy for Charles I and been dispossessed by Cromwell on that account, and banished? And had not another fought and died under Sarsfield in the siege of Limerick? But the Catholic Marie, whose father was a British officer, was beloved of her Protestant Magan cousins; and her uncle, Val Hussey-Walsh, the lawyer and Ulster King of Arms, was held in no less regard and affection, as also were the other Catholic cousins, the Dwyer brothers. Perhaps it is religion itself, rather than those caught up in its web, that has something to look to and something to answer for. Have the seven deadly sins ever caused as much accumulated and tumultuous disquiet in the world as has religion itself – at least the three religions of Judean origin?

While I was at The Downs we had outbreaks of both chickenpox and mumps, the one causing acute irritation, the other a good deal of pain. We were confined to bed in our dormitories, but felt aggrieved because we nevertheless had to do our lessons instead of being treated with the delicacy which we deemed proper for suffering invalids.

We also had another, and much more serious, outbreak. I think it was towards the end of November 1918 that we were struck by the Spanish 'flu, perhaps the most vicious 'flu virus ever. It killed many more millions of people in a few weeks than all the casualties of the war. I think I was the first boy in the school to get it, although it had already been widely reported and people were not therefore caught unawares.

I suddenly felt very unwell, and said so. I was put to bed, and within half an hour was unconscious. It is a demonstrable fact that I recovered. Many other boys got it, and we were considered very lucky to have no deaths in the school. But I do not think it was only luck. I think we were very well looked after by the staff. We were kept in bed until fully recovered, and no risks were taken with us. And I recall in particular that we were told that the indications elsewhere were that eating was dangerous, and that we must therefore just patiently accept the fact that we would be given very little food until we were considered to be well on the road to recovery. The fact that it was a highly dangerous illness could not be kept from us. There were too many people dying for it to be hidden. Moreover, it was probably better that we should know in order to engender our willing and sensible co-operation in the treatment prescribed for us.

The month of November 1918, brought not only the Spanish 'flu but also the end of World War I.

11 November 1918 was a dead still, leaden, autumn day. It must have been in the short break just before lunch that I was outside doing something or other, when a messenger-boy from the village on a bicycle, with some goods for the school, arrived, bursting with news.

There being no radio or television in those days, we got our information from newspapers, rumour and gossip; and much was left to the imagination. If memory serves me right, the higher class newspapers, *The Times* for instance, were far above stooping to anything so vulgar as having pictures. At all events, when the boy appeared through the school gates out of the murk, he immediately and eagerly addressed me:

''Eard the news?'

'No. What news?'

'Armistice.'

'What is that?' It was a new word to me, and to him, but he was palpably proud to be able to elucidate.

'End of the war,' he replied. 'Fightin' stopped at eleven o'clock this morning. Not peace, see. Fightin' stopped; just arguin' now.'

Now turned harbinger myself, I rushed into the school and, with as knowledgeable a mien as I could assume on the meaning of an armistice, broke the news. It elicited gratifying interest, dampened only by some syntactical correction of too closely verbatim a rendering of the messenger-boy's tidings.

I do not, however, think that we felt elation, just a negative relief that the burden and anxieties of war had been lifted from us. All else temporarily remained the same. We were all, even we children, numb and war-weary after four years of deprivation, food shortage and casualties on a scale that had left none of us untouched. We were past imagining what beneficial changes peace might bring to our day-to-day lives.

Chapter 13

Wartime: Holidays

While the Great War lasted, I had four periods of holiday from my prep-school. The first was the eight weeks summer holidays from late July to late September 1917. We went back to Ireland and spent the holidays at Killyon Manor. Nine years of age, I was free to come and go as I pleased. There was a five hundred acre home farm there in the midst of a much larger estate.

The house was very primitive, but we did not mind that. The conditions were not uncommon in houses in Ireland at that time. The place had not been renovated since the mid-nineteenth century. There was only one water closet and no bathroom. We bathed in tin tubs. There was no boiler for heating water, which had to be heated on the kitchen range. There were water tanks in the roof but all the water had to be pumped up there by hand from a hand pump in the kitchen yard. There was no automatic pump and, of course, no mains water – and no main drainage either. Only wood was burnt in the kitchen range – no coal. The wood was all fallen timber from the estate.

At the beginning of the holidays, we took off our shoes and stockings and spent the whole holidays in bare feet. The soles of our feet became so hard that we could run about on the gravel in front of the house without discomfort.

Mollie and I spent much time with the farm hands and the gardeners, involving ourselves in harvesting and anything else they were doing, and no doubt getting in the way, but they were very patient with us. And we learnt a thing or two. One day, when we went into the cattle yard, there was some activity going on in one of the

146

stalls. We went over to see what it was all about. No-one stopped us. Why should they? They were country folk in tune with nature. Their own children did not have to close their eyes to the facts of life. And so, what we witnessed was a calf being born.

But our greatest interest was the river. It ran a hundred yards from the house – the river Deal, a tributary of the Boyne. We bathed in it and fished it, but best of all was the beautiful horse-shoe weir, a little below the house. Except in high flood, the water running off the weir and down the sloping stone apron at the foot of it was seldom more than shin deep. It was therefore perfectly safe to paddle about there. The only danger spots were the sluice gates each side of the weir through which a heavy volume of water always poured at high speed, but it was a danger that was easily avoided. Below the weir the river was wide and shallow, and the whole area was a source of endless interest and pleasure to paddling children; and Mollie and I spent much time there.

One of the chief excitements was catching perch – a coarse fish, but quite edible. A spawning instinct brought them upstream and they tried to climb the weir. They could not get beyond the foot of it, and were then washed back down the apron. We could see them dash up through the foam, and we had a few seconds to run through the water and try to catch them before they fell back into the river. Some days we caught quite a lot. Joe, the hunchback who worked in the three acre walled garden and was a life-long friend of ours, particularly liked them, and we used to swap them with him for tomatoes. He was a real Irish character and we were immensely fond of him. Long after we were grown up and he had retired from Killyon, we used to visit him in his cottage. He never married. He kept a little shop in his house in which he sold small things of use to his neighbours – boxes of matches and so forth.

Mollie was so fond of the old weir that, when she was dying, she asked that her ashes might be scattered there. The present charming owner, Mrs Diana Purcell, not only agreed but also planted a weeping willow tree there in Moll's memory.

There was another interest to which we could always turn if tired of whatever else we had been doing – hunting for the jewels. The

The weir at Killyon in winter

The weir at Killyon in summer

eccentric old female cousin, Augusta Magan, whose will had brought disaster to the family estates, had, in one of her fits of barminess in the previous century, turned all the staff out of the place and hidden the family jewels. They have not been found to this day, but we hopefully hunted for them when we had nothing better to do. Our searches were not altogether in vain. It is curious how some things of value can remain undisturbed for a very long time. Mollie one day found hanging behind a shutter in the old ballroom two fine, heavy, silver, meat skewers. Why did anyone hang them behind a shutter? Had they been there for a hundred years? I still use them as paper knives.

Not long ago, in the next parish to mine in England, a public-spirited parishioner undertook to clean the church floor. He brought along his Hoover. Vigorously working it over the floor he suddenly heard a rattle in its works. Thinking he had picked up a nail, he decided to empty it. What he found was a gold half-sovereign dated 1776. How on earth had it escaped notice on the floor of the church for perhaps two hundred years?

All too soon, the Killyon holiday of the summer of 1917 was over and we went back to London. A great advantage of holidaying in Ireland then was the abundance of good country food there – plenty of meat, eggs, vegetables and fruit; no shortage of bread; and perch, eels and a few trout out of the river.

In London where we spent the next two holidays – Christmas 1917 and Easter 1918 – it was very different. Up to the middle of 1917, the German submarine blockade of Britain was increasingly successful. Food became progressively shorter, and there was no rationing system until mid-1917. As children in London in the holidays, we spent much of our time searching for food. So short was it that I recall a triumphant day when one of us managed to buy a couple of fish, which meant welcome fish-pie for a few days.

At school they managed to feed us pretty well. I think that in or near the country, there was more to be had than in the middle of a city. I do not remember many details, but I recall that fresh eggs were all but unobtainable. We had scrambled eggs made from a dried egg powder. I enjoyed it. We did not have ordinary sausages, but we did have a form of sausage meat with a not very agreeable taste. I do not remember any shortage of bread, and there was certainly some butter – or perhaps margarine – and jam, mostly plum and apple. The whole nation, including the armed forces, became sick – in so far as anyone could become sick of any food – of plum and apple jam. Perhaps they were the most abundant home-grown fruits. Quite a lot of parents managed to send the boys cakes and they were always shared, so we not infrequently had cake for tea.

In London, we were allowed to wander about at will. We were not very far from Hyde Park and Kensington Gardens, and I enjoyed going there and running about and playing. I did things I had never done before. I went to the British Museum, the Science Museum, the Tower of London, Madame Tussaud's, and other such interesting places, and found it all endlessly fascinating. I was particularly interested in the Zoo and the Natural History Museum because Aunt Vera Biddulph's father, Sir William Flower, had been the Chairman of both. I was sometimes taken to tea with his widow, Lady Flower, a marvellously venerable old person in her nineties. She was of special interest to me because she had known Queen Victoria and had met many of the crowned heads of Europe.

In London, too, I went to the theatre. I saw *Peter Pan*, and *Chu Chin Chow*, and enjoyed them both greatly. I was also taken to see a play called *Daddy Longlegs*. It bored me. I think it was above my head.

For an Irish country boy, London had a curious affect on me. It bewitched me. I fell in love with it. For someone brought up on the wild beauty of Lough Ree and the lovely old demesne of Killyon Manor with its river and its weir, it was strange that, as a nine-year-old boy, I would climb the steps of the Albert Memorial and drink in the beauty of the view eastwards to Whitehall. Of course there were frustrations. I could not rush about and throw stones in the streets, but there were unexpected compensations which have continued to serve me for a lifetime.

We had some relations and family friends in London, and we visited their houses. There were, too, some children's parties; though what they found to give us to eat, I cannot now imagine. Nearly all the houses in central London are now offices, but at the time of which I am writing they were all private houses.

We also got to know some of our neighbours. I recall a very distressing tea-party with one of them. When I arrived, the lady of the house was alone with three or four children, younger than me. We had tea in the dining-room. Her husband was not there. During tea she produced a bent and battered silver cigarette case and asked me to have a look at it. Then she broke down. She told me that it had belonged to her seventeen-year-old eldest son who had joined the Royal Flying Corps and been killed on a training flight. The other children sat passive, eating their tea, but she was inconsolable.

There were striking differences between London then and London now. Tarmac roads were not the rule. Experiments were being made to improve on the rolled stone chips and cobbled roads. One experiment that caught on was the use of wooden blocks, about the size of a brick, with which many streets were paved for a long time. They were clean, quiet and comfortable. Much, perhaps most, of the traffic was still horse drawn. The hansom cab – called a 'growler' – was more frequently used than taxis. There were taxis, but during the First War they were run on gas supplied from a gas-bag on the roof. Men still earned a living as porters carrying heavy loads through the streets. Goods were mostly carried on horse-drawn drays. The omnibuses were open on the top deck, and you either put up your umbrella, if you had one, or got wet, if it rained. There were also coal-fired steam buses run by Thomas Tilling and Company.

The fact that most of the houses in central London were private dwellings caused their owners to be particularly concerned to keep them smart. Door handles and door knockers were well polished and shone brightly. Another means of giving a house a smart appearance was to whiten the steps. Thus the streets in the early morning would present a vista of maids' bottoms as they knelt on the steps whitening them.

There was a familiar cry that rang through the early morning streets – 'Milk-o!'- the milkman on his rounds. Milk was not bottled. The milkman had a pony and cart and milk churns. The maids came running up the basement steps with jugs into which the milkman ladled the milk with long-handled pint measures. The milkmen had an amorous reputation, and it used to be said that half the children of London bore a strong resemblance to the milkman, a canard that those worthies would no doubt have vigorously refuted.

Another daily sight was the coalmen. Houses depended for their cooking and much of their heating on coal and coke, though there were also gas fires. The coalmen would come down the streets early in the day with large horse-drawn drays piled with bags of coal. In front of each house was a round cast-iron cover let into the pavement which led to the coal hole below. The coal men would lift the covers and shoot the coal out of the bags through the hole. The empty bags were always neatly stacked at the back end of the dray.

As dusk fell in the evening another public benefactor appeared to perform his office: the lighting-up man. Street lights were gas. On each lamp there was a moving arm with a ring suspended at each end, and there was a pilot light in each lamp. To light the lamp, the arm was pulled down in one direction. To extinguish it, it was pulled down in the other. The lamp-lighter had a wooden pole with a hook on the end and, as darkness fell, he would walk through the streets pulling down the arms with his hook to light the lights. In the morning he did the journey in reverse to put out the lights. Most domestic lighting in houses was also gas, not electricity.

Later, when my father was given a command in Norfolk, we moved from London to a very nice house on the outskirts of King's Lynn. As a boy interested in history, I was fascinated to be living on the edge of such a lovely interesting ancient English country town. King's Lynn is particularly famed for its ancient markets.

At King's Lynn, the local estate owners invited my father to their shoots, and one day he brought me back from a Sandringham shoot the case of a cartridge which had been fired by King George V - a much treasured object thereafter.

During the time that we were at King's Lynn, the fifth and youngest child of my parents was born, my brother Francis. I was particularly pleased to have a brother. My father was unable to be at his christening in one of the great King's Lynn churches. A heavy responsibility therefore fell on me - a nine-year-old boy at the time. My mother, being deaf, did not notice, when it came to naming the child, that the parson was giving it the wrong names. My recollection is that the parson, too, was deaf. At all events, I took upon myself the responsibility of stopping the service and insisting on an 'as you were'. I do not know whether an 'as you were' really does the trick at a christening. If not, the Recording Angel is the only person who knows my brother's other names.

In King's Lynn, we continued the practice of not having meals with our parents. My brother Francis's starched nurse presided over our meals. One day at lunch my sister Sheelagh threw a loaf of bread at me. I retaliated by emptying a jug of water over her. We were sent in disgrace, I bruised, she dripping wet, to the dining-room to confess our misdemeanours to our parents. We were given penitential occupation weeding the drive.

The nurse was a keen supporter of the Salvation Army and used to take Mollie and me to their services. We loved them, with all the cheerful hymns and songs and music, and I think instruments like tambourines. General Booth, the founder, had said that he did not see why the devil should have all the best tunes. We used to visit the house of a lovely Salvation Army man and his motherly wife whom we adored and with whom we had marvellous teas with apple pie.

Chapter 14

Post-war: Preparatory School, 1919-22

The end of the war brought a changing world for me. At prep school our headmaster, Mr F.E. Chappell, was released from the army, and returned to us, and we were very soon moved from The Downs. He bought a famous old school, Parkside, at Ewell, Surrey. It was a lovely place, standing in some ten acres of ground in beautiful rural surroundings, perhaps a mile or so from Ewell which was then a very small village. The school had ample dormitory space, good classrooms, a fine panelled dining-room and its own consecrated chapel, which was particularly endearing to me as I was a keen chorister. The headmaster himself took the services and played the organ. We had choral services morning and evening.

The spacious wooden army huts were moved to Parkside from The Downs. One of them became a boxing-ring and carpenter's shop, the other a roller-skating rink, which was a splendid addition to our amenities. The school had its own walled garden which must have provided most of our vegetables.

And there was another most exciting and agreeable innovation. Mr Chappell got married. Marion, his wife, was only half his age. He was forty-one and I think she was not yet twenty-one, but she was as competent and responsible as she was lovely and lovable. There was room for everyone in the warmth of her affections and she was a mother to us all. It is little wonder that I look back on my prep school days as among the most agreeable of my life. Marion lived to be ninety-four.

It was in that year, 1919, following the end of the war, that I developed appendicitis. I was taken to a hospital in Croydon, and

155

there operated on and left with an enormous scar. I can still vividly recall the horrible experience of being smothered into insensibility with chloroform and ether, the only form of general anaesthetics known at that time. But the hospital was agreeable, and there was a very nice little girl patient who had had pneumonia, whom I found an enjoyable companion. She was an only child and had been terribly ill and her poor parents were frantic because they thought she was going to die. They were very friendly, and nice and encouraging to me.

While I was still in bed, my father came one day to visit me. He had been to a levee at Buckingham Palace that morning to receive a CMG from the hands of King George V for his war services. I recall my fascination with the beautiful enamel work on the badge of the Order.

I suppose the problems of staffing a school were still acute in the immediate post-war years but, whatever they were, they brought two heroic figures into our life. One was a man in his sixties who had retired from the Indian Civil Service. That made him a person of interest from whom we could draw stories of life in the Orient to stimulate our young imaginations and to widen our horizons. But to us boys, he had an even more heroic attribute than that. In true Empire-administering Olympian tradition, he was a former Oxford blue – an Association Football blue. We did not expect him to perform as he had done in his youth, but he was patently very knowledgeable about football, and was still well able to teach us useful lessons in ball control, not least the match-winning skills of accurate cannon-ball shots at goal. Blues in those days were real heroes to us.

The other heroic figure who joined the school staff was a very young-looking graduate straight down from Cambridge, another blue, this time for hockey. Young boys can seldom be taught hockey as well as we were by him; and he had another asset – a source of first-class, but cheap, hockey sticks. So, in addition to being well-taught, we were well-armed with excellent weapons.

Perhaps it was due to his influence that the headmaster took those of us who were in the hockey team to see the Oxford and Cambridge

- the Varsity - hockey match when it was played not far away, I think at Sutton. I remember Mr Chappell saying, as the Cambridge team arrived in their light blue blazers: 'I would have given my eyes to have been qualified to wear one of those when I was young.'

A curious incident took place during the match. We were standing behind the Oxford goal. Cambridge were pressing, and one of them took a shot at goal from close quarters. The Oxford goal-keeper hit the ball hard back and it struck a Cambridge man on the forehead, knocked him down, and bounced back into the goal. A richly deserved goal I thought. But the referee thought differently. When the Cambridge man had picked himself up and was restored, the referee gave a free hit against him for 'handling' the ball. I thought that very harsh.

It was in 1919, the year after the 1st World War ended, that the school moved from The Downs, Purley, to Parkside, Ewell. Fighting had ceased on 11 November 1918, and 11 November 1919 became the first 'Armistice Day' anniversary on which the whole nation honoured her dead with two minutes' silence of remembrance at 11 a.m.

It so happened that my father had spent the night of 10 November in the school and, on that first Armistice anniversary morning next day, Mr Chappell allowed me to go to see him off from Worcester Park railway station - at that time little more than a wooded wayside halt - not far from the school.

While we waited for the train, the clock struck eleven, and the sirens, for the first time, sounded for the two minutes' silence. My father and I and the porter who, of course, had also been in the Armed Forces during the war - the only people on the platform - stood side by side at attention until the all-clear siren ended the to me seemingly interminable two minutes.

My father then broke the silence with a sort of valediction to the world at large:

'Four years; and a lot of good pals gone west.'

At that moment, the little two-carriage steam train drew in, and a small boy remained alone on the platform waving good-bye.

Despite my maternal grandmother's prediction that my father would not be able to compete in life because of his lack of formal education, he succeeded very well as a temporary soldier. He reached the rank of lieutenant-colonel, was three times mentioned in dispatches and awarded a CMG. But perhaps most significant and telling of all, the twenty-five officers serving under him clubbed together to give him a retirement present of a fine silver salver with each of their signatures engraved on it – and he was still only thirty-eight years old when his military service came to an end. He was offered an appointment as a brigadier-general to stay on but, like most temporary officers, he felt that he must get back to his own civilian work and life.

Ewell is near Epsom, and we felt ourselves enveloped in some of the euphoria of Derby Day. There was more traffic on the road that ran past the school gate and there was a general air of interest and excitement, but we were never taken to the Downs to see the race. One year, however, 1921 perhaps, it had been decided for the first time ever to control the traffic from the air, and to that end a beautiful airship, the R34, was employed. How successful it may have been at traffic control, I do not know, but it was an unforgettably marvellous experience to have that enormous and lovely machine manoeuvering low above us for a large part of the day.

Wednesdays and Saturdays were half-holidays. We played games every day except Sundays, but matches against other schools were played only on half-holidays.

One Wednesday afternoon we were due to play an away match and Mr Chappell was chivvying those of us in the team out of the dining-hall after lunch to get us there on time. At that moment someone handed him a telegram which he immediately opened and read. A little later, one of the other boys asked me, as we were on our way to the match, whether I had seen Mr Chappell's face when he read the telegram. He said he had turned very pale, and he wondered what was the matter. I had not noticed anything. But we were to learn what it was about when we got back to school.

One of our number, John Booth, had died. He was a weekly boarder. He had gone home for the week-end and had contracted pneumonia. We knew he was not well because he had not returned to school on Monday, but that was all. It was before the days of antibiotics, and pneumonia was a very serious and dangerous illness.

John Booth was a charming, gentle, civilized person and was a close friend of mine. He was a good artist and had just begun painting in oils.

A few of the more senior boys were allowed to volunteer to go to his funeral. Back in the mental atmosphere of my old Oldcourt wall perch, I was both attracted and repelled at the thought of John's funeral, but I volunteered and went. I can still see his coffin and sense the anonymity of that box which housed his hardly imaginable mortal remains.

There was one boy in the school, Jerry Bryant, who was the nephew of one of the *Punch* artists of that time. He drew like Raphael, and with extraordinary speed and fluency. I enjoyed drawing, but became so well aware that my pedestrian efforts could never come within a hundred miles of matching Jerry's that I gave it up.

We were, of course, taught English, but I do not recall any special literary encouragement. We did not, for instance, have a school magazine. But there was one boy, Kinsey, who seemed to have an extraordinary budding literary gift. His father was a professional photographer, so perhaps he lived against an artistically creative background. At all events he kept us enthralled with the never ending saga of an extraordinary character with the wonderful name Lara Gudge. Lara Gudge was hardly either male or female. He, she or it was humanity personified. He, she or it both enjoyed and suffered every experience that might befall anyone, including rather chronic indigestion.

Why did we never hear again in later life of two such talented people as Jerry Bryant and Kinsey? I hope it was not because they did not survive the health hazards of those days. Jerry, even at that time, was a delicate person.

Mr Chappell kept a horse which I used to ride. Marion Chappell kept two white nanny goats, friendly, amusing, intelligent and mischievous creatures which gave a large amount of milk. We were allowed to keep pets, and I kept white, and white and black, mice. What happened to their numerous progeny I no longer remember. We also collected caterpillars and were able to watch the whole cycle of cocoon, chrysalis and emerging butterfly or moth. We were not taught any biology or botany, or indeed any of the sciences.

Sunday was different from other days. Because we were living at a time when children were heavily indoctrinated with religion, Sunday had to have something of a sacred, if not penitential, air about it. We wore different clothes. We had to dress in black 'Eton jackets' with striped trousers and stiff white collars. I think we were allowed back into more comfortable garb after lunch. We had Divinity classes and three choral services in the chapel, early morning, 11 a.m. and evening, instead of the normal daily two in early morning and evening. We went for an awful walk in the afternoon, instead of games. The full details I no longer remember, but there was enough excess of sabbatarianism, and it was a boring enough day, to sow seeds of at least a little agnosticism in some of our young hearts and minds. Two pluses, however, there were: one for the body, the other for the soul. When food became more plentiful after the war, there was always a roast, with roast potatoes, for lunch. We looked forward to that. The other inestimable benefit was that we were allowed to play only one game on Sunday, chess, so we all became chess players. It is one of the few pastimes - painting is another - in which it is possible to become so absorbed as to lose all sense of time.

In the Christmas holidays of 1921, the last holidays before my final term at Parkside, Mr and Mrs Chappell took me and another boy - I remember all his names: Anthony Gordon Hepple (Tony) Marr - to Villars in Switzerland for a fortnight. As there was no commercial flying in those days, we went by boat across the Channel and then by train across France, all of which was very interesting and exciting as I had never been abroad before; and especially because we had to change trains in Paris and cross Paris from one station to another.

I do not know what Villars is like now - possibly a large winter-sports resort - but then it was a very small village with one large hotel where we stayed. There was a funicular railway, but there were in those days no chair lifts, cable cars and so on. The philosophy of the time, too, was that good things must not come too easily. You had to work for your fun. So we did not use the railway. If we wanted the joy of whizzing downhill on skis, we must first earn it by plodding up-hill. That was tedious, particularly as Tony and I were not allowed to use ski sticks as Mr Chappell thought them dangerous. However, the exhilaration of coming downhill was such, once we had gained a little competence in skiing, that it was well worth the uphill plods.

One day I was on the nursery slopes when a man came up to me shuffling along on skis and said:

'I'm new to these things, can you tell me how to use them?'

Feeling very inadequate and incompetent myself, I nevertheless felt that I must try to reveal such little knowledge as I had acquired. I told him he must keep his legs together, and not let them fly apart, and that he must keep his skis parallel, like this; and I set off to give him a demonstration. First there was a gentle slope, down which I made satisfactory progress; then the hill dropped steeply and I disappeared from the view of my pupil and promptly fell over unseen. I dusted the snow off myself and returned to receive his gratitude for the demonstration, after which I had the elevated satisfaction, from my superior station as mentor, of watching him falling about for the next quarter of an hour.

The hotel tennis courts were flooded, and re-flooded every evening to make an ice skating rink, and my greatest satisfaction of all in Switzerland was watching the elegant ice dancing by expert skaters on the illuminated rink at night. Being long before the days of television, I had never witnessed such a thing before.

Our last day at Villars was marred by tragedy. I had been mesmerised by the hotel proprietor, because he wore a beard which was not fashionable in those days, and he was always in evidence, busy about the hotel.

That last morning there was a thaw, and when the proprietor was making some examination of the exterior of the hotel, a two foot long icicle broke off the roof, went straight through his head and killed him instantly. Had we not departed that day, I would no doubt have been a volunteer to attend his funeral.

On our return journey to England, we spent a night in Paris. During the afternoon Marion Chappell took Tony and me out; we became inadvertently parted from her in the metro and were lost. We went out into the street, and I recognized it from some wild duck that I had seen hanging outside a butcher's shop when we had driven through it that morning. Such is the receptiveness of children's minds that we were able to find our way back to our hotel from other such landmarks as we had noticed during our drive there earlier in the day.

I think Tony Marr had no father. Perhaps he had been killed in the war. But his mother was later to acquire universal fame under her *nom de guerre*, Constance Spry.

I left Parkside to go on to my public school at the end of the Easter term, 1922. Fred and Marion Chappell gave me a little book which I still have – *Stories from Dickens*. On the cover, embossed in gold, is the school crest, a feline/canine creature known to us as the 'puss-dog'. On the fly-leaf, in Fred Chappell's handwriting, is written:

Bill Magan
A little souvenir of a very happy association – 1917-1922,
and with very best wishes for the future from his friends
F.E.C. & M.C.

The association was not to end there. It was too real and too close for that. Like marriage, it was to go on, 'till death do us part'. I was still in touch, and in correspondence, with Fred Chappell when I was past seventy years of age. He lived to a few weeks short of his hundredth birthday, and remained as lively as ever to the end.

Long years after I had left the school, he said to me one day: 'You must call me "Fred".'

'No,' I replied. 'Impossible. You could never be anything but "Sir" to me.'

In his ninety-seventh year, he published a small book of sparkling, amusing light topical verse. Here is a brief sample:

THE GOALKEEPER'S LAMENT
By F.E. Chappell

I don't want to grouse, but it does not seem right,
And I think you'll agree when I tell you my plight.

162

I'm the goalie and therefore claim, much to my pride,
It's through me that the cup has been won by our side.
Now, when one of our lads kicks a goal, he is faced
By the rest of the team, except me, and embraced,
But when I stop a hot one, although the crowd claps,
There are no hugs for me from the rest of the chaps,
And a barrage of toilet rolls, thrown by some thugs,
Is poor substitute for some kisses and hugs.
The Captain must treat me much better or else 'e
Will find I'm a transfer, and playing for Chelsea.

Is there any wonder that I had a life-long affection for such a schoolmaster?

My first Commanding Officer lived to ninety-eight. Was the longevity of my early mentors due to the fact that I gave them so little trouble?!

Chapter 15

Post-War Holidays: Life in Ireland

The other major part of the changing post-war world for me was our return to live in Ireland. My father could not wait to pick up the threads of his Irish life, and I think he managed to get an early demobilisation from the Army. But life was going to be different from his expectations. We were not going back to Oldcourt at Athlone. I was never again going to sit on my funeral wall. My grandmother would go on living in Ardaghcourt on the eastern outskirts of Athlone, so the town and the area would continue to be very familiar to me.

A friend of my father's, however, Charlie Norton, who had inherited from his father a malting business, P.R. Norton & Co., was short of good senior management and offered my father a directorship if he would join the company as an executive director and help to run it. My father agreed, and Charlie Norton invited him to live in the mill house at one of the company's properties, Levitstown on the river Barrow, four miles south of Athy in the County Kildare. It was also convenient for Charlie because he lived only a few miles further south in a very nice house on the outskirts of Carlow.

Charlie Norton was married but had no children and he always seemed to me to be rather a crusty old fellow. He was also very religious and said grace at his meals with his wife. He also was fond of his food. His wife used to let the cook off on Sunday evenings and she and Charlie would have a cold supper which Charlie did not much like, so he had a special grace for that meal: 'Thank God for what the cook will allow us on Sunday evening.'

While the mill house at Levitstown was being put in order for us, we lived for some months at Uncle Middleton Biddulph's beautiful house, Rathrobin. He and Aunt Vera were away. I spent one holiday there. The house I enjoyed, not least the billiard room – though I never developed into a skilled billiards player – and the library where I found masses of interesting books even to an eleven-year-old boy as I then was. I enjoyed the luxurious sensation of being in the panelled library, and also the panelled dining-room. The panelling was unusual. It was teak, brought back from Burma by Uncle Middleton when he was serving there in the Army. A lovely room was Aunt Vera's very bright and feminine drawing room with watercolours by David Cox and other well-known artists.

Always interested in pictures, I enjoyed, too, Uncle Middleton's good, if not famous, collection which decorated the house and gave it distinction. The family had been acquiring pictures over a period of two hundred years. Most of the pictures were lost when the IRA bombed and burnt the house in 1923.

In one important respect I enjoyed Rathrobin less than our other old family home, Killyon Manor. There was no river at Rathrobin – only a small lake. There was plenty of interest in the Rathrobin farm and, the straw ricks being full of rats, I, together with Uncle Middleton's terrier Risk, became an expert ratter, but it was no substitute for playing and paddling and fishing at the weir at Killyon. Whenever I subsequently visited Rathrobin, Risk always gave me an impassioned greeting and, in effect, as I supposed, invited me to go ratting.

In those days the corn was threshed in a large mobile piece of machinery called a 'Thrashing Mill'. It was towed into position beside the corn ricks by a traction engine, a large steam engine which also drove the mill with a driving belt. In Ireland they were commonly called thrashing engines. As the corn stacks were gradually demolished and the corn fed into the mill, out came the rats, and that was when Risk and I reaped our main rat harvest.

In addition to Rathrobin, another family home was maliciously destroyed. My paternal grandmother was a member of the Richards family. In 1921, the IRA burnt the Richards' family home, Ardemine House, Gorey, Co. Wexford, with the whole of its valuable contents.

The mill at Levitstown was a handsome old stone building which looked like a castle, its flat roof having a crenellated surround. It was a tall building, six or seven storeys, but large enough and wide enough not to look disproportionately high.

Levitstown was an altogether fascinating place. The mill house was not very large, but was big enough, with a bit of a squeeze, to accommodate the family, our father and mother, and five children; three indoor servants, a cook, kitchen-maid and house-maid; and a governess for the younger children; and there was a spare room for guests. There was a dining-room, a drawing-room, a study; and a school-room for the younger children. In the back – west – wing of the house, were the kitchen premises – kitchen, pantry, larder, dairy and maids' bedrooms. There was only one bathroom in the house, and two lavatories, one of them outside.

The house stood within a few yards of the river, quite a large river which ran to the west of it. Much of the river Barrow was navigable for barges, but the two mile up-stream stretch from our house had a series of shallow rapids and, to circumvent that, a canal had been built which ran the other side of our house beyond the drive and roadway to the mill. The canal was six or eight feet above the level of

The mill at Levitstown, Co. Kildare

the river, and it re-joined the river through a lock at our mill. From there on, the barge traffic went south using the river again.

The canal was not a busy commercial highway. For us it was a very pleasant additional amenity to the river. I suppose it carried an average of three or four barges daily, some of them still horse-drawn, others with simple diesel engines which propelled them at about walking pace. The Irish barges are as long as the English narrow-boats, but are much wider, and the canals are comparably broader.

With all that water, interesting activity with the lock being filled and emptied, the bargee community whom I got to know and for whom I would work the lock, and endless boating and fishing, the place was paradise for a thirteen-year-old boy. A friend of my father's, Hew (short for Hewitt) Barrington-Jellett, gave me a canoe that he had had as a boy. If you learn to manage boats when you are young, you become very skilled. The boat, like a bicycle, or a horse for that matter, becomes an extension of yourself. I was able to hold a boat absolutely still in fast running water with a pole, a paddle or oars, while my father or mother or someone else fished with a dryfly.

Mollie and I had a very nice mongrel dog called Rex, but it had one defect. It killed chickens. My father said we must get rid of it, so we decided to offer it to one of our bargee friends. He said he would be delighted to have it, but we warned him that it killed chickens. 'Oh,' he said, 'that's great. Now I'll never go short of a supper.' Whenever the barge passed our way Rex would give us a rapturous greeting.

We always kept dogs. They were mainly for shooting, but were of course close friends of the family as well.

Bell was a pure-bred Irish water-spaniel. She was a very gentle dog with an equable temperament, very well mannered and at the same time a polished and very efficient retriever. She went out into the bushes to die alone on the morning of the day that I left home to go and join my Regiment in India.

Dinski was a mongrel spaniel, a cheerful and ebullient dog and very companionable, also immensely brave. He belonged to my sister Maureen who brought him into the family.

Sweep was a cross between an Irish water-spaniel and a black

Labrador. She was jet black with a curly coat. She was almost human, and only lacked the power of speech, but could articulate in other ways. She attached herself to Mollie and me, or other members of the family, in whatever we were doing. One thing she loved was swimming races with us across the river. She was as much at home in the water as she was on land and was a first-rate retriever.

We had our own ducks and geese, which lived on the river all day, but came into their pens in the stable yard, a hundred yards from the house, at night. The yard had a coach-house that housed my father's car – there was only one car in the family. There were two loose boxes, one of which housed my mother's hunter, and the other a horse ridden by my sisters; and there was an old pony named Diamond which had belonged to my uncle Bertie Biddulph when he was a boy. We kept cows for our own milk, and chickens for eggs and to eat.

My mother, ever since she was a very young girl, had been interested in and enjoyed dairy work, and had had her own dairy. As a child she had won numerous prizes for dairy products. Our various moves during the war had precluded her from having a dairy, but now at Levitstown she was able to re-establish it and she did all the dairy work herself including keeping all the utensils scrupulously clean.

Some of the milk from our cows was poured into jugs and used for normal household purposes. It was, of course, unpasteurised. The remainder of the milk – the bulk of it – was poured into large flat enamel pans in the dairy and allowed to settle and the cream to come to the top. The cream was then skimmed off with perforated concave discs into earthenware jars leaving a residue of skim milk which was fed to calves and pigs or sold to the cottagers who had many uses for it. Once a week the cream was poured into the wooden churn which my mother churned by hand to make the week's supply of butter. Some of the cream was allowed to go sour and my mother made cream cheese from it. It was always served decorated with a nettle. The residue of the cream after the butter had been churned from it was known as butter-milk and was used to make bread. It was supposed to be very good for us to drink it, but it was sour and we did not like it. Butter was never served at table in a lump. My mother patted it into little balls and curls with a pair of serrated 'butter pats'. It was always decorated with parsley. Junket – known to us as 'curds' – was another frequent and favourite spin-off from the dairying activities.

Water for the house and the mill was pumped out of the canal by a mechanical ram. Water for drinking was brought daily in galvanised buckets from a well in a nearby field. Many fields in Ireland were, like that one, known as the 'well-field'. We had a rose-garden, flower garden and vegetable garden.

All the outside work was done by one man, Paddy Whittaker. He did the gardening, looked after the animals, milked the cows, fetched the water from the well-field and washed my father's car.

Although my mother greatly enjoyed hunting, she kept only one horse, a good one, and hunted one day a week or, at most, three days a fortnight, always with the Queen's County Hounds who drew some of her father's old coverts.

At Levitstown we were not far from Kilkea Castle where lived the elderly aunts and uncles of the Duke of Leinster, Lord Frederick and Lord Walter Fitzgerald, and the Ladies Nesta and Alice Fitzgerald. They were lovely people and they let my father shoot over their estate of several thousand acres. It was all wild shooting. They kept only one keeper, Willie English, and did not put down any pheasants or have organised pheasant or partridge shoots. My father and Willie English shot snipe by the dozen, woodcock, a few duck and teal, golden plover and pigeons, and I used to take part in the winter holidays from school.

During the winter holidays, too, we always spent a few days at Killyon Manor and shot there. The keeper there, unlike Lord Frederick Fitzgerald's keeper, never carried a gun on shooting days. At Killyon we did drive the pheasants out of the woods, and there were also a few grouse on the red Blackshade Bog, and the ubiquitous – for Ireland – snipe, duck and teal. We were, of course, very familiar with walking the bogs; trying to stalk wild geese in the evenings, I learnt to pick my way across quaking bogs even when the light was almost gone.

The Christmas holidays always meant a visit to my grandmother at Ardaghcourt, Athlone, and a couple of days shooting on my father's lovely former estate in Roscommon: more snipe and duck, and in

169

particular golden plover flighting at dusk. Golden plover coming fast downwind in the dusk are a challenge to even the best of shots.

In effect we did little or none of what might be called social shooting - half a dozen or more guns, more or less well dressed, shooting reared pheasants. That, too, calls for good shots and skills of its own and my father was very good at it, but what he liked best, and what we did most of, was in effect hunting wild game. We were hunters hunting it in its own rugged habitat. We were always wet to the knees even when we had to crunch through ice, and I was not infrequently wet to the waist. We would shoot till dark, the last shoot being duck or golden plover flighting. We would then seek the warmth and hospitality of some friendly cottage, some family who had known my father since he was a boy very likely, probably his and his father's former tenants, and there we would change into dry clothes. My fingers were often so cold that I was struggling to undo buttons with the knuckles of my thumbs. Gloves, of course, were not allowed; they were for softies. We could, however, wear mittens.

My father's companions were Arthur Handcock, until he grew too old, and then Hew Barrington-Jellett. The day's work done, we would drive in an open motor-car to wherever we were spending the night - closed cars were a rarity. My father and Hew would be in the front of the car talking their heads off. I would be curled up on the back seat with a very wet dog, trying to keep each other warm. It all amounted to an upbringing of automatic hardihood and self-reliance. I enjoyed it all immensely at the time, and comparable shooting expeditions later on elsewhere in the world. But came the day, very many years ago, when I tired - indeed sickened - of killing these beautiful and interesting creatures, and gave up shooting for ever.

There is no logic in it. I eat pheasant with relish when my friends are kind enough to give me a brace. It is just a matter of sentiment. Shooting is a very satisfying skill for those whose sentiment has not turned against it. It is a direct source of a good deal of employment, and also of other skills such as gun-making. It is a source of protein in the diet of a good many people. And there is the paradox that it also conserves and preserves game that would otherwise disappear, or at any rate greatly decrease. Where I now live, my garden is full of pheasants and partridges. That would not be so but for the fact that I live in the middle of a shoot.

My mother had fished all her life, mainly on the Slieve Bloom mountain streams near her home in the King's County. My father had not been a fisherman before the war, principally because, having been brought up near that great Shannon Lake, Lough Ree, he had, together with two of his sisters, Violet and Rachel, devoted his free time in the summer to sailing. However, at Levitstown he took to fishing and became a successful fisherman. Except for my eldest sister, Sheelagh, we all fished at Levitstown, including the youngest member of the family, our brother Francis.

My Mother in 1938

My sister Mollie and I, being inseparable friends, constantly boated and fished together. On the Barrow we caught perch and pike, and trout on a dry-fly only. We all became expert dry-fly fishers and could land our fly on a sixpence – as the saying is. There were also some old quarry holes not far from us where we caught roach and rudd. And the kindly Fitzgerald lords and ladies at Kilkea Castle allowed us to fish their delightful little wet-fly trout river, the Greese, which ran right under the castle walls.

Willie English, the keeper, used to be told by the kitchen at the castle to bring in so many trout for lunch, and he always caught whatever was needed. He had an extraordinary knack at catching those little trout. Sometimes, I used to fish with him. He always caught twice as many fish as I did, even when we used exactly the same flies. Wet-fly fishing is fished normally downstream, and you take a step downstream after each cast. One day I said to Willie:

'It's not fair. You are fishing downstream of me so of course you are catching more fish.'

'All right,' he said. 'We'll change places, and I will fish upstream behind you.'

We did that, and he fished only one cast behind me, but he continued to catch twice as many fish.

The secret was the 'strike', so called – the moment when the fish takes the fly and you tighten the line. Willie said I was a fraction of a second too late. He had attuned his eyes to seeing the fish under water and he 'struck' gently the moment it took the fly. I only saw the fish a moment later – when it rose.

Fishing takes one into lovely places and is a fascinating pastime. I never supposed that I would give it up but, like shooting, I have long since also abandoned fishing.

There was a pond in our garden but with so much water about we did not need the amenity of the pond, so we got the agreement of our parents to fill it in and build a grass tennis court. My sisters Mollie and Maureen and I carted soil from I do not recall where and filled in the pond, and I erected a fence round the court. We had to mow it and keep it marked, and look after it ourselves and, although none of us were skilful tennis players, we made good use of it; although we

In my canoe

did not have many neighbours, we were able to arrange a few tennis parties.

Another sort of party which my mother loved, and which indeed we all enjoyed, were cross-country paper chases. They took place in the Easter holidays, and we would try to get up to twenty people involved.

At one time we had a young maid named Nellie – a feather-headed young thing of about eighteen. When my parents were out, or not obviously in evidence, she would come to me and plead:

'Master Bill. Will you take me out for an oar?'

'Of course, Nellie, come on,' and we would run down to the pier, she in her uniform, black dress, white apron and white cap, and we would jump into the punt.

'Now, Nellie,' I would say, 'hold on tight, and make yourself comfortable,' and I would push off. The subsequent proceedings were routine and predictable.

I would row gently out into the river, and sedately up-stream.

'Now, Nellie, are you enjoying yourself?'

'Yes, Master Bill.'

'Well, just relax and admire the scenery.'

Then, I would 'catch a crab' and lose one of the oars overboard. I would begin pulling wildly with the other oar and the boat would go round in circles, with Nellie screaming and me crying out:

'Nellie, we'll never get home. We'll be drownded.'

Then I would go into reverse and back-paddle and the boat would go round in circles the other way. Then, in the confusion, I would lose the other oar overboard. More screams, more predictions of disaster. Then I would say:

'Nellie, I've a brainwave – the stretcher.'

I would pull it out – the footboard – and begin paddling furiously with it in pursuit of the oars, which were floating away from us down-stream. But then, disaster of disasters, the footboard would slip out of my hand, lost overboard as well as the oars, and at that moment I would grab Nellie's cap and throw that overboard as well.

All was then utter confusion, pandemonium, and screams and shouts, and I would begin rowing the boat with my hands, rocking it violently, splashing water all over the place, making sure that Nellie got plenty of it.

Of course, I was so used to the boats that I was in total control in any circumstances, and soon Nellie's cap, the footboard and the oars were retrieved, and we rowed back to the landing stage where Nellie, distinctly wet and rather dishevelled, jumped out and ran back to the house saying:

'If the Mistress catches me, she'll kill me.'

I thought it was much more likely she'd kill me. Anyway, we were never caught, and Nellie retained an insatiable appetite for being 'taken out for an oar'.

The mill at Levitstown, Co. Kildare

P.R. Norton & Co. decided to diversify at Levitstown at the time that we went there. Half the mill continued to be used as a malting – the half beside our garden. The other half – the half beside the canal – was to be used to manufacture cattle cake. My father loved engineering and he greatly enjoyed the process of converting half the mill for manufacture. The chief source of power for the manufacturing process was water. He installed a water turbine near the canal lock, the source of its power being the difference in level between the canal and the river which gave a strong flow of water to revolve the turbine blades at high speed. The principal purpose of the turbine was to run an electric generator. We therefore had something which, in those days in country districts of Ireland, albeit in a somewhat crude form, was an unusual luxury – electricity.

As the mill had, as I have said, six or seven floors, the process of manufacture of the cattle cake was worked out on a clever gravitational system. The raw materials were raised onto the appropriate floors in sacks through a series of double flap trap doors and then decanted into, and descended through, and were mixed in, a series of hoppers until, finally cooked in coke ovens on the ground floor, it came out as warm, moulded, nuggets of cattle cake. I have long since forgotten the ingredients, but two of them were locust (carob) beans and molasses; the cake tasted sweet, and was no doubt agreeable to cattle. We heard endless talk from my father of proteins, carbohydrates, sugars and so on. I think most of the cake was bought by local farmers whose carts were always waiting at the mill entrance while being loaded.

After the harvest was threshed, the farmers brought in the malting barley which was spread out on the wooden floors and went through the malting process, which included being turned by hand with flat wooden spades, and was dried in the kiln. My chief recollection of malt is its delicious biscuity smell.

In the spring, seed barley and fertilizers were sold to the farmers. All these goings on and the connection with the farming community made life interesting and gave it something of a bustling purpose, as did the coming and going of the workpeople, all of whom of course we knew intimately.

One very good family friend came out of it all, a young Dublin architect, Toby Miller, who lived on a house-boat on the canal while seeing to all the construction needs related to installing the turbine and the cattle cake manufacturing arrangements. He remained a close and very dear family friend until his all too untimely death.

The mill generator provided electricity for the house. There was no battery system to store the electricity; it was a direct supply from the generator and was a bit 'flickering'. Its wattage was limited, but it produced enough power for an electric motor to lift the sacks in the mill, and to run a Hoover and one or two electric fires in our house as well as the electric light. My father was afraid of the possibility of a bearing in the generator heating if it was left running all night, so it was my job when I was at home to run out to the mill last thing at night and shut down the flow of water to the turbine, and stop the whole thing. After that, if anyone wanted a light, it had to be a candle or a torch.

It was the time of the post-war rebellion in Ireland against British rule – 1919-21. There was much inconvenience and some danger. The disruption of roads was the worst inconvenience. As I have said, bridges were blown up and trees felled to block roads. And I have told of the burning of my great-uncle Middleton Biddulph's beautiful house, Rathrobin, and of the attempt to murder my aunt Violet Magan. We took as little notice of the conditions as we could, but sometimes, for instance on his business travels, my father thought it prudent to go armed and if I went with him, I carried his revolver on my lap. When Uncle Middleton learnt that I thus escorted my father on his visits to Rathrobin to help my Aunt Violet to run the estate there, he sent me £100 – riches in those days which, safely invested, brought me in a welcome income, perhaps the equivalent of £150 or more today.

When, in 1921, the twenty-six southernmost, and mainly, Catholic counties became independent and known as the Irish Free State, the terms of the agreement were not radical enough for the more extreme nationalists, who therefore then began a civil war against the new Free State leaders, some of the most able, prominent and liberal of whom they murdered. At all events, we continued for some years more to live in what today would be called 'terrorist conditions'. But human beings are remarkably adaptable. We adjusted ourselves to the circumstances and ignored them as far as possible, and carried on our lives as best we could, which was a pretty good best on the whole.

There being no radio or television, and living a long way from places of entertainment such as cinemas, we made our own amusements. Our doctor, John Kilbride – Dr John – who lived on the outskirts of the town of Athy, four miles to the north of us, was a pianist, and he would sometimes come in the evenings and play duets with my mother on her violin, and there would be songs round the piano. Often in the evenings my father and mother and Mollie and I played bridge – auction bridge, because contract bridge had not then been invented. My father indulged in endless post mortems for which there was ample scope since my mother was a hopeless card player. The post mortems were thus as ineffective as they were tedious. Mollie and I played a lot of bezique and cribbage, both of which I think were games of pure chance, so we had equal opportunities. Our eldest sister Sheelagh never joined in these pastimes. She remained a loner. Maureen and Francis were at that time too young. Of course we read a great deal.

There was not a very active social life. Families like ours were too few and too scattered in that part of Ireland, and the motor-car had not reached anything like the universality of later times.

There were many splendid local characters. The Dooly family lived in the lock house and were traditionally the lock keepers. One of them, Tom Dooly, became the foreman at the mill. He was typical of the skilful, dextrous and ingenious people who are often to be found in Ireland. He himself largely installed all the new machinery in the mill, and when he decided to marry, he built a new house and did the whole of the construction with his own hands. He was tragically killed by a fall from his bicycle.

His relative, Ned Dooly, was a most attractive man. When I was not at home, he was my father's boatman for fishing. He also worked in the mill. He knew that I knew that he surreptitiously smoked a short pipe at work when no-one was looking, and I never gave him away. Smoking was strictly forbidden, and rightly so, as the whole of the inside of the mill, all the floors and partitions and the props and pillars holding up the floors were timber and as dry as matchwood. The mill was indeed, and most unfortunately for such a beautiful old building, burnt down, but after our time at Levitstown.

I cannot fill these pages with local characters, but I cannot omit Biddy Nolan. The driveway to Levitstown House was, I suppose, a couple of hundred yards long. It was approached by a drawbridge over the canal. In effect, we lived on an island. Across the drawbridge, fifty yards or so onwards and at right angles to it, ran the Athy-Carlow road, and straight on across it, the road to Kilkea. That area was known as 'the Cross' – short for cross-roads. There were some cottages there, and in one of them lived Biddy Nolan, who was our washer-woman. She came up to the house I think a couple of times a week to do the washing and ironing. She was a most lovable person, a real Mrs Tiggywinkle and, as children, we adored her. She sang quaint songs:

'As I was goin' to a fair in Athy
I saw a petticoat hanging to dry.
I took off me old breeches and hung them nearby,
To keep the petticoat waar-um.'

That song seemed to have some topical point because she was the proud possessor of an ass and cart and in it she rattled off to Athy every Thursday to do her shopping.

Clothes washing in the home was all done by hand. There were no automatic washing or drying machines. The chief item of equipment was a large tub full of soapsuds – indeed the place used to smell of soapsuds. The second item was a 'scrubbing board' – a corrugated wooden board perhaps 3 feet long by 18 inches wide on which the wet clothes were rubbed with friction. The third piece of equipment was a mangle. It had two rollers set close together between which the wet clothes were pressed to wring out the water. The mangle was, of course, worked by hand. It did not dry the clothes completely. They were finally dried on a 'washing line' outside, and on a rack hanging from the kitchen ceiling.

Biddy's husband must, I think, have been long since dead, but she had one daughter, married, who lived in another of the cottages at The Cross. Then there came Biddy's lodger, a distant relative of some sort, the kind of person who is liable to turn up in Ireland. He had spent his life in America. In our local country surroundings he appeared a complete fish out of water. He always wore a suit and a very well cared-for trilby hat, unlike the customary battered head-gear in Ireland; he had about him an air of dull and fragile respectability. I do not know whether anyone ever learnt his name. He was generally known as 'the retired American'. How, after a lifetime in America, he stood the primitive conditions of Biddy's cottage, I do not know.

Not only Biddy, but the other servants too were very much our friends, and I spent a great deal of time in the kitchen, not just getting in the way but willingly doing useful jobs, and being rewarded with the agreeable right to lick the bowls. Although there was a cook and a kitchen maid, the mistress of the house in those days took a close interest in her kitchen and could herself cook and make cakes and jam and so on. The main work was done in the kitchen in the morning, and my mother would be there part of the time. In the afternoon the cook had a rest. She was going to have to cook dinner later on.

Throughout the winter we usually had game for dinner, and rabbit was a frequent lunchtime staple. My mother had a few specialities which she thought good for our health, among them nettle soup and dishes made from carrageen moss, an edible red seaweed. It is named after Carragheen near Waterford in Ireland where it grows profusely. It is also known as 'Irish moss'.

Despite our homemade electricity at Levitstown, there was no electric cooker and no electrical gadgets: no electric kettles or toasters. There was still an enormous, black, coal-fired kitchen range which was the only source of heating for many purposes, including heating the bath water for the one bathroom. The cook had to be an expert at manipulating a series of flues to keep the ovens at the temperatures she needed. The fire in the range had, as in the old days in Oldcourt, to be allowed to go out at night. The ash had to be cleared out next morning early and the fire re-laid and lit, and the range polished with 'blacking'.

Our chief mode of personal transport was the bicycle. We did not have the modern, light-weight, multi-speed bicycles. Some of them had three-speed gears, but we did not have that luxury. Nevertheless, our cycles were good, strong and useful machines. They were our normal means of transport for almost all purposes locally, and even for longer journeys. There were times when Mollie and I cycled to Killyon Manor, forty-five miles away in Co. Meath. There was very little traffic. We could cycle the four miles to Athy, which we often did, without ever meeting a motor car. There would be a few ass-carts, and the occasional dog-cart, so called, a distinctive sort of trap which, with a good horse, could average 12 m.p.h. Sometimes we would have to ride through droves of cattle or sheep, going to or from markets. The roads were awful, full of pot-holes, dusty in summer and muddy in winter.

As I suppose has been common with children ever since the bicycle was invented, I also enjoyed taking the edge off myself just whizzing around aimlessly on my bike.

Being a Protestant family, we followed the conventions common at that time. We went to Matins on Sunday mornings either at the church in Athy, of which my father was for a time a churchwarden, or at the little church at the gates of Kilkea Castle to which, in fine weather, the Fitzgerald lords and ladies walked down the castle avenue. I do not recall that we ever attended Evensong. Perhaps they did not have it in those country churches, which did not have a choir.

Sunday, just as before the war, continued to be a day of restricted pleasures but now that we were older, our outdoor activities were neither curtailed nor supervised so, so long as we went to church, we could otherwise go where we liked and do what we liked during the rest of the day, even if we could not touch a pack of cards indoors. It is hard now to understand why cards should be innocent on week-days and wicked on Sundays.

From time to time interesting guests came to stay. One such was our 17th/21st Lancer cousin, Reggie Boothby. He was a clever eccentric, a fine linguist, and a good writer. He had been brought up in

Reggie Boothby

Scotland. What claim he had to be eligible to wear a tartan I do not know, but on the occasion of his visit to us he seemed concerned to underline his Scottish background. He wore a kilt all the time, and marched up and down in front of the house on the sweep playing the bagpipes.

My father thought it an absurd performance, and he also loathed the bagpipes and threatened to shoot Reggie who, being a brave fellow and probably not much scared about being shot, did not, however, want his precious bagpipes punctured. He therefore withdrew to a more distant field where he played them to the astonishment of the cows which gathered round him in a goggling half-circle but otherwise, unlike my father, refrained from menacing him.

Boyhood comes to an end with adolescence, so, as I was now approaching that period of life, it is time to end this account of my boyhood. I hope the story is enough to suggest what life was like for a child growing up in Ireland in the years immediately before, during and after World War I, in an old Irish Ascendancy family which was changing with the times. The father had sold his landed estate, and taken largely to business, while he and his wife and family nevertheless continued to follow and enjoy the conventional country sports and pursuits traditional to such families, and while we still had an old, if rather tumble-down, Irish mansion as a second home.

I hope, too, that the story throws some light on the reason why an Irish childhood causes our toes to grow roots in Ireland. The southern Irish are not British. They do not feel themselves to be British. Their culture is still strongly underpinned by ancient Picto-Celtic influences.

The cultural atmosphere in which we grew up in Ireland was therefore very different from the background to an English upbringing. The patience, warmth and kindliness of all those – not least the affectionate women – who influenced our childhood, their eloquence – never at a loss for a word – and their amusing drolleries, are among the foremost recollections that glow in our hearts in our autumn years.